Solomon's New Men

Solomon's New Men
The Emergence of Ancient Israel as a National State

E. W. HEATON

Pica Press
NEW YORK

For Josephine and Nicholas
who say it is their turn

Published in the United States of America in
1974 by PICA PRESS
Distributed by Universe Books
381 Park Avenue South, New York, N.Y. 10016

Library of Congress Catalog Card Number: 74-13412

ISBN *0-87663-714-4*

Printed and bound in Great Britain

Contents

Preface

Writing this book has given me the kind of pleasure I experienced twenty years ago when I ventured to produce a general work entitled *Everyday Life in Old Testament Times*. Although I am now attempting to present the culture of a particular age to a more sophisticated audience, the work has proceeded, as before, by asking direct (and sometimes unusual) questions about how things actually worked in antiquity and by seeking answers in a range of specialized studies much too diverse to allow any but the polymath to feel securely at home. The measure of my indebtedness is indicated in fairly extensive bibliographical notes, which (since they are tucked away at the back of the volume) the reader may ignore or consult at his pleasure. I hope, however, that some of my fellow students will find them of interest and judge whether I am right in thinking that the argument of these chapters is novel only in the sense that it brings together and inter-relates a miscellany of scholarly investigation which has been building up during the last decade.

The pleasure of trespassing in the carefully-cultivated plots of one's academic colleagues is, of course, inseparable from the risk of being dismissed as a bungling intruder. In particular, I must rely on the tolerant understanding of professional Egyptologists. It soon became clear to me that Israel's rapid development in the age of Solomon owed much to the mature civilization of Egypt and this line of enquiry led me to the Griffith Institute and, from there, to an adventure in a wholly new world. It was a world, however, of whose language I was (and remain) unhappily ignorant. Although

Dr J. W. B. Barns, who was Professor of Egyptology at Oxford until his recent death, read much of my material and gave me generous encouragement, blemishes such as inconsistencies in the transcription of proper names and the absence of diacritical marks (quite apart from other and, perhaps, more grievous solecisms) clearly expose my amateur status.

It would be absurd for an amateur to criticize the quality of the English translations of Egyptian texts, but the reader should be warned that they are quoted here exactly as I found them and that they often use an archaic idiom and a sentence structure which make literary appreciation unusually difficult. In addition to Adolf Erman's invaluable collection of texts, recently re-issued in an inexpensive edition with a very useful introduction by William K. Simpson (*The Ancient Egyptians*, Harper Torchbooks, 1966), the newcomer to these studies now has *The Literature of Ancient Egypt*, edited by William K. Simpson (Yale, 1972; new and enlarged edition 1973), which provides an excellent selection of stories, instructions and poetry, freshly translated and lucidly annotated. Unfortunately, this work appeared too late for me to adopt its version in quotations.

I owe many debts. At the kind (and courageous) invitation of Dr Brian Heeney, Master of Champlain College in the University of Trent, I recently enjoyed the instructive privilege of presenting the theme of these chapters to a Canadian audience drawn from a wide range of academic disciplines. During my absence in Ontario, Mr P. G. Atkinson of St John's College (one of many Oxford pupils who have patiently borne their tutor's immoderate enthusiasm for scribes) generously checked a number of references in the Ashmolean Library. From the outset, the book has greatly profited by the sustained encouragement of Professor Christopher Brooke, the General Editor, and since it has been in the hands of the publishers it has been much improved by the perceptive criticism of members of their editorial staff.
The Deanery, Durham.   E. W. HEATON

Solomon's New Men

Prologue

THE TRANSFORMATION of an ancient tribal society into a sophisticated national state within less than a century is itself a phenomenon sufficiently remarkable to merit investigation. When that ancient people is Israel and the political and cultural revolution involved is one which profoundly shaped the literature and thought of the Old Testament, the subject assumes an interest which is more than merely antiquarian.

Israel's emergence as a fully-fledged state was effected with astonishing rapidity. Saul, its first king, hardly provided more than a backcloth for the drama. In addition to the fact that he was a manic depressive, his roots were so firmly embedded in the old tribal tradition that radical change would have been abhorrent. For this reason, his reign of twenty-odd years succeeded only in exposing his country's anachronistic organization and the mounting pressures which were soon to force it to come to terms with the superior culture and military power of its neighbours.

Israel's break with her past was delayed, therefore, until about 1000 B C, when a freebooting mercenary of enormous energy and even greater ambition secured the kingship and began the task of dragging his subjects screaming into the first millennium. All the clichés about men destined for their hour, in David's case, ring true. Here was a military genius in control of a small but crucial sector of the Middle East at a time when the old imperial powers – Egyptian, Hittite and Assyrian – were more or less in a state of collapse. David seized his opportunity with vigour and during a reign of forty years' hard campaigning transformed an incoherent complex of tribal territories into a united international power.

David's military and political achievement, like all empires before and since, would have simply disappeared in the slipstream of history had it not been for a side-effect totally devoid of glory and glamour. Israel soon discovered that a highly-centralized state cannot be run without a civil service and that a civil service cannot be maintained without schools to train its recruits. And schools, however pedestrian the aims of their founders, lead sooner or later to new ways of thinking. How far David himself encouraged a new educated class in Israel is difficult to judge, but there is no doubt that enormous progress was made by Solomon, his son and successor.

This book is an attempt to explore the documentary and archaeological evidence for Solomon's systematic exploitation of his father's legacy. It is argued that Solomon's 'new men', educated primarily to staff a bureaucracy which grew up almost overnight, were the key to the speed and character of this final phase of Israel's development and that, moreover, they were deeply influenced by the long-established civil service of Egypt. It was through the bureaucrats of Jerusalem that the 'wisdom' of Egypt, upon which its scribal meritocracy had been nurtured for centuries, first gained entrance to Israel and began to shape its institutions, literature and intellectual life.

The influence of educated men in Israel is only just beginning to gain recognition from students of the Old Testament, partly, it seems, because they have been taught to avoid reading back into the ancient world their own presuppositions. The surprisingly 'modern' outlook of the literature of Solomon's age suggests, however, that this danger has been greatly exaggerated. In fact, one of the most fascinating conclusions to be drawn from a study of scribal education in Egypt and Israel is that it inculcated a cast of mind which is still dominant in our own bureaucratic society. If the educated élite of Israel exercised an influence on their nation's thinking at all comparable to that of the middle classes in the modern west (and the idea is by no means absurd), a great deal of Old Testament scholarship is at present missing the point.

This book, of course, makes no claim to pursue all the far-reaching questions raised by its theme, since its scope is confined to the seventy years during which Israel first emerged to join the mainstream of the civilized world. Thus, the first chapter reviews the annals of Solomon's reign with the aim of indicating in general terms that both his policy and the style in which his scribes presented it are best understood as a conscious imitation of the imperial tradition of the Pharaohs. This grandiose and pathetically short-lived ambition would have been inconceivable without the economic resources and psychological impetus provided by David's military conquests and so, in the second chapter, these are briefly sketched. In the third chapter, the new bureaucracy created by Solomon is compared with the well-established pattern of administration maintained by the scribes of Egypt. The fourth chapter passes under review the extensive public works (including the Jerusalem temple) which witness to the range and complexity of the scribal administration demanded by Solomon's *folie de grandeur* and investigates the economic and cultural resources upon which he was able to draw. The somewhat meagre evidence for scribal education is presented in the fifth chapter and an attempt is made to demonstrate that the biblical book of Proverbs betrays a modest middle-class ethos and was probably used in the training of candidates for Israel's civil service. Apart from the book of Proverbs and the Annals of Solomon, the only contemporary evidence which actually survives of the new social climate consists of three short literary works now tucked away in the first few books of the Old Testament – the Joseph Story, the Succession Story and the so-called Yahwist's History. These lively and mature compositions are analysed in the sixth chapter and compared with their Egyptian counterparts. Since Egyptian civilization had dominated the whole of

Syria–Palestine for a large part of the second millennium B C, it is relevant to enquire in the concluding chapter whether its influence on emergent Israel was encountered indirectly (and, perhaps, fortuitously) through the immediate Syrian cultural environment, or whether Solomon adopted Egyptian models deliberately and directly from the court of the Pharaohs.

From beginning to end, in every department of Solomon's bold enterprise, whether it was building new towns or collecting the money to pay for them, administering a province or servicing the corps of chariotry, compiling lists or writing books, his civil servants were working in the background as the self-effacing agents of a revolutionary and irreversible change. They left an intellectual and literary legacy which was continuing to shape the mind of Israel long after their master's Pharaonic pretensions had been dismissed as a lamentable aberration.

The Annals of Solomon

NOTHING remotely resembling the record of Solomon's reign is to be found elsewhere in the Old Testament. Characteristically, the history of other Hebrew kings is either summarized, like that of Omri, in a few laconic verses,[1] or presented obliquely, like that of Ahab, in a loose narrative recounting the religious, political and military activity of his period.[2] By contrast, the Annals of Solomon, from which I Kings 3–11 claim to be no more than an extract,[3] are sharply focused, detailed and entirely domestic – an adulatory record of the king's spectacular achievement, from which all the tensions, crises and failures of his reign, and with them its personal and significantly historical dimensions, have been deliberately omitted. In consequence, Solomon emerges from this unique biblical encomium as little more than a faceless wonder.

A number of passages in the Annals are immediately identifiable by their theological bias as the contribution of the later deuteronomic writer who embodied the record in his history of the Hebrew monarchy;[4] otherwise, the material of these chapters has a good claim to be accepted as the work of the professional scribes of Solomon's court. Indeed, the bulk of it appears to derive directly from their official archives. Thus, we are presented with a list of the king's principal officers and regional governors (4.1–19); a memorandum of the provisioning arrangements for the palace and the army (4.22–28); an embellished version of the agreement made with Tyre for the supply of building timber (5.1–18; 9.10–14); a detailed and quite secular description of the Temple building, its decoration and fittings (6.2–10, 15–38; 7.13–47); an account of the construction of the palace and other royal buildings in Jerusalem (7.1–12); a note of the royal cities built outside Jerusalem (9.15–19); an item about foreign captives and their reduction to perpetual forced labour (9.20–23); a record of the establishment of a merchant fleet in the Red Sea (9.26–28); and a miscellaneous catalogue of trading and other royal enterprises intended to redound to Solomon's greater glory (10.14–29).

The beginning and end of the Annals, however, present material of a different kind. In contrast to the impersonal archival style which flattens the rest of the record, the inaugural dream and judgment of Solomon at the beginning (3.4–28), like the visit of the Queen of Sheba at the end (10.1–13), are vividly-sketched vignettes. It would be a mistake to conclude that this difference in style necessarily indicates a difference in provenance. To judge by Egyptian precedents, the professional scribes of Solomon's court would have been as adept in portraying dramatic scenes as in compiling administrative data and, as educated men charged with executive tasks, would not have differentiated as sharply as we are tempted to do between 'cultural' and 'practical' expertise. They were innocent of the distinction between what our academic jargon calls 'pure' and 'applied'. To them, *all expertise was wisdom* – the wisdom required for government and the administration of justice,[5] the wisdom manifested in the affluence of the court,[6] the wisdom represented by the bargain with Tyre,[7] and the wisdom displayed in the learning of the schools,[8] upon which, ultimately, nearly all wisdom was thought to depend.

The attenuated modern view of wisdom as analytic insight detached from executive power was quite foreign to the outlook of the ancient world. Not only the Annals of Solomon, but the Old Testament as a whole authentically reflects its cultural milieu when it uses a single term for the wisdom of the craftsman,[9] the wisdom of the king,[10] the wisdom of his royal counsellors,[11] and the wisdom of the

16

I Painting from the Theban tomb of the Chief Treasurer of Tuthmosis IV (Dynasty XVIII). We have to imagine the Pharaoh enthroned on the left, as the Chief Treasurer presents the Syrian tribute-bearers. Among the gifts are an exotic ointment horn decorated with a woman's head and an open hand, a bow-case, jars of blue glaze and a rhyton shaped like a bird.

2 Sandstone stela (height 30·5 cm.) from Amarna of Amenophis III and Tiy, his queen (Dynasty XVIII). Portrayed with the new 'realism' of the Amarna age, they sit at a table piled high with offerings, the obese king languid in a long, loose robe.

3 Painting from the tomb of two Theban sculptors (Dynasty XVIII). The male guests in the upper register indicate their high official rank by holding a papyrus sceptre. In the lower register, the ladies feast in a separate room. Nude girls anoint their wigs with cones of scented fat. Under a chair, a charming cat waits for scraps.

4 The east wall of the First Court of the temple of Ramesses III at Medinet Habu (Dynasty XX), displaying the records of the Libyan War of Year 11.

Creator,[12] since all these in their different capacities were thought of as exercising expert mastery over recalcitrant raw material and shaping it to their own design. Throughout the ancient Near East wisdom was basically 'know-how', the fruit of long experience and professional apprenticeship. It enabled a man to size up a situation, sort out its complexities and select a course of action which was both desirable and practicable. The prophet Ezekiel, in his famous condemnation of the king of Tyre, clearly illustrates the fundamental character of wisdom as the kind of expertise which produces the goods:

> By your wisdom and your understanding
> you have amassed wealth for yourself,
> you have amassed gold and silver in your treasuries;
> by great wisdom in your trading
> you have heaped up riches,
> and with your riches your arrogance has grown.[13]

This is a fair description of the wisdom of Solomon as the Annals present it, and there can be little doubt that it was primarily sheer professionalism that his scribes were employed to promote and praise.

THE VISIT OF THE QUEEN OF SHEBA

The court legend of the official visit of the Queen of Sheba, to take the last story first, probably reflects a commercial mission (see pp. 61–62), but it is recounted primarily to illustrate the claim of the royal scribes that 'men of all races came to listen to the wisdom of Solomon, and from all the kings of the earth who had heard of his wisdom he received gifts.'[14] Courtesy visits and the ceremonial exchange of costly gifts were the immemorial preoccupation of royal houses in the Ancient Near East and precedents for the theme of this legend abound in the records of Egypt. For example, that remarkable file of correspondence in Akkadian now known as the Amarna Letters, which, for the most part, were addressed to the Pharaoh between 1387 and 1362 BC by his eastern allies and Syrian vassals, reveals a quite obsessive concern with the acquisition of luxurious status symbols;[15] and the no less remarkable series of commemorative scarabs issued during the first twelve years of the reign of Amenophis III (1417–1379 BC) makes it clear that the Pharaoh's scribes had little to learn about what the current euphemism calls 'public relations'. One of these royal press-releases reports the arrival in Egypt of the daughter of the king of Mitanni, accompanied by a retinue of three hundred and seventeen ladies and attendants so marvellous as to merit the issuing of a communiqué to all the Pharaoh's loyal subjects.[16] In many ways, Amenophis III was to Egypt what Solomon was to Israel – the heir to unparalleled military conquests, who chose to expend his vast resources on the pursuit of luxury and display. It is true that Solomon could not boast an enormous pleasure lake, like the one Amenophis III made for his queen Tiy and publicized in the last of his scarabs,[17] but, nevertheless, the style of living at the court in Jerusalem was such as to leave even the fabulous Southern Queen breathless in admiration: 'When the queen of Sheba saw all the wisdom of Solomon, the house which he had built, the food on his table, the courtiers sitting round him, and his attendants standing behind in their livery, his cupbearers, and the whole-offerings which he used to offer in the house of the Lord, there was no more spirit left in her.'[18]

Equally breathtaking was the wisdom displayed in the king's universal knowledge: 'Solomon answered all her questions; not one of them was too abstruse for the king to answer.'[19] No esoteric insight into divine mysteries is being claimed here, but, rather, a professional mastery of the encyclopedic learning of the schools, such as we find in the texts used by Egyptian scribes in teaching their pupils.[20] In addition to the egregious adulation of the court scribes, such a claim discloses that robust confidence in the infinite possibilities of education characteristic of any developing meritocracy; and this argues strongly for its early date, since later Old Testament writers came to represent knowledge of the natural order, like that of Solomon, as a mysterious wisdom reserved for God alone, man's wisdom then being confined to the sphere of religious and moral obedience.[21] The only feature of the story of the Queen of Sheba which betrays the hand of a later editor is the reference to the divine election of Israel, as evidence by Solomon's succession to the throne in order 'to maintain law and justice'.[22]

THE INAUGURAL DREAM AT GIBEON

The interpretation of Solomon's wisdom as being essentially a divine gift for the administration of justice almost completely dominates the present account of the king's inaugural dream at Gibeon.[23] In view of its close resemblance in ideas and terminology to a passage in the first chapter of Deuteronomy, which describes Moses' choice of 'men of wisdom, understanding, and repute' for the administration of justice, it has been suggested that everything in the story, except the vestiges of an account of a dream theophany followed by the offering of sacrifice, derives from the later deuteronomic historian.[24] This view is improbable. Dream theophanies associated with the building of sanctuaries are found, it is true, throughout the literature of the Ancient Near East and it is not inconceivable, as recent scholars have suggested, that the 'Sphinx Stela' of Tuthmosis IV (1424–1417 BC) reflects an Egyptian tradition upon which the scribes of Solomon might well have drawn. It recounts how in a dream the young Tuthmosis was nominated Pharaoh by the god of the sphinx, received his request to care for his image, and proceeded immediately to offer sacrifice in the city sanctuary.[25] However, the theophanies to Tuthmosis and Solomon are totally dissimilar except in their bare narrative framework and, on general grounds, it seems likely that the original content of Solomon's dream included a divine promise of wisdom for the task of successful government, which the later deuteronomic historian reinterpreted narrowly and moralistically as wisdom for the administration of justice. Indeed, it is probable that the content of the original promise may be discerned in what the editor self-consciously *dismisses*: 'Because you have asked for this, and not for long life for yourself, or for wealth, or for the lives of your enemies, but have asked for discernment in administering justice, I grant your request.'[26] With this as a clue, a connection with the Egyptian scribal tradition, at once more central and more secure than that offered by the Sphinx Stela, immediately suggests itself.

The Pharaohs, as is well known, were much addicted to the practice of covering the walls of their temples with compendious accounts of their magnificent achievements. One such inscription, slavishly copied by a whole succession of rulers, takes the form of an address by Ptah, the god of Memphis, to Ramesses II (1304–1237 BC). In this remarkable document, Ptah promises Ramesses everything an ambitious potentate could possibly desire – happiness, wisdom, power, wealth, foreign labour for building projects, long life, the subjection of his enemies, and even a state visit from the king of the Hittites in order to present to the Pharaoh not only gifts but the hand of his eldest daughter in marriage.[27] It is reasonable to speculate that it is some such stereotyped Egyptian convention which the deuteronomic historian is dismissing and that what he is dismissing he actually found in the narrative of his original source. It is not difficult to see that Solomon's endowment with 'a heart so wise and so understanding that there has been none like you before your time nor will be after you' is very similar to the wisdom which Ptah promises to Ramesses: 'I make thy heart divine like me, I choose thee, I weigh thee, I prepare thee, that thy heart may discern, that thy utterance may be profitable. There is nothing whatever which thou does not know, [for] I have completed thee this day and before, that thou mayest make all men live by thy instruction.'[28]

Confirmation of the Egyptian tradition as the source of the original narrative is provided by two significant points of detail. Solomon's prayer for 'a heart with skill to listen, so that he may govern thy people justly and distinguish good from evil' echoes a highly characteristic feature of the teaching of the Egyptian scribes. For example, in the *Instruction of Ptahhotep*, the earliest extant specimen of this didactic genre. from about 2350 BC, the 'hearing' of the pupil is presented in word-play as the essential qualification for his future task of 'hearing' judicial cases – that judgment between 'good and evil' for which a ruler pre-eminently needed to be equipped: 'To hear is of advantage for a son who hearkens. If hearing enters into a hearkener, the hearkener becomes a hearer.'[29] To this extent, the deuteronomic historian's interpretation of Solomon's wisdom as *judicial* wisdom was far from being an innovation. Similarly, the idiom used to describe Solomon's lack of experience in government – 'I do not know how to go out or come in' – is drawn directly from Egyptian court protocol, as the following stereotyped description of one of the multifarious duties of the Vizier clearly suggests: 'The going out of all that goes out of the king's-house shall be reported to him; and the coming in of all that comes into the king's-house shall be reported to him. Now, as for everything going in [and] everything going out on the floor of the court, they shall go out [and] they shall go in through his messenger, who shall cause [them] to go in [and] go out.'[30] Just as the address of Ptah to Ramesses II began with a legend of the Pharaoh's divine origin and status,[31] so, we may suppose, the Annals of Solomon began with a legend of the king's divine endowment with wisdom for government. The diffident form of the present narrative may reflect controversy about the legitimacy of Solomon's succession,[32] or, more simply, the awareness of his scribes that his policy of emulating the traditional imperial role of Egypt was a daring innovation for which a recently-established monarchy stood in need of divine credentials. Later Israelite scribes used an analogous form to accredit the innovating work of Moses and Jeremiah.[33]

THE JUDGMENT OF SOLOMON

The neat little narrative of the Judgment of Solomon, which follows his inaugural dream, has analogies throughout the repertoire of eastern folk-lore and continues to defy the efforts of scholars to trace its origin.[34] The closest known parallel appears to be a version from India, where the two women are presented as wives of a deceased merchant competing for the rights of inheritance, which were denied to a childless widow. The preoccupation of the teaching of the book of Proverbs with prostitutes[35] and the comparable story of David's judgment in the fictitious case of the two sons of the widow of Tekoah[36] suggest the possibility that the biblical version was a variant current in the circle of Solomon's scribes. Although it appears to owe its present position at the beginning of the Annals to the later deuteronomic editor, who used it to illustrate his moralistic thesis that Solomon 'had the wisdom of God within him to administer justice',[37] the story actually invites the reader's admiration for the king's perspicacity and knowledge of human nature – of precisely the kind that had been complacently claimed over the centuries by the scribes of the Egyptian court. Intef, the Herald of Tuthmosis II (1504–1450 B C), for example, boasted that he possessed to the full just these qualities:

The only wise, equipped with knowledge . . . giving attention to hear the man of truth . . . understanding the heart, knowing the thoughts, when nothing has come forth from the lips . . . turning his face to him that speaks the truth, disregarding him that speaks lies . . . giving attention to hear petitions . . . free from partiality, justifying the just, chastising the guilty for his guilt, servant of the poor, father of the fatherless. . . .[38]

It is evident that Solomon's scribes were heirs to a well-established court tradition.

CONVENTIONS OF THE COURT SCRIBES

It is probable, indeed, that the scribal tradition of Egypt

underlies not only the prologue and epilogue of Solomon's Annals, but the pattern of the record as a whole. A marked degree of similarity in content and idiom between the Annals and the Address of Ptah to Ramesses II has already been noted and their common features are found equally in a larger composition written in praise of Ramesses III (1198–1166 BC) with the explicit purpose of winning support for his son and successor, Ramesses IV (1166–1160 BC). Known to us through the Great Harris Papyrus, now in the possession of the British Museum and reckoned the most magnificent of the Egyptian state archives, it gives a detailed and laudatory account of all the Pharaoh's benefactions and mighty deeds during a reign of thirty-one years. This voluminous document was evidently compiled hastily on the Pharaoh's death from the records of the three main Egyptian temples – at Thebes, Heliopolis, and Memphis – and is presented in three separate sections, each constructed on the same pattern though written by a different scribal hand. The Theban section, for example, describes the building and equipment of the great temple of Medinet Habu and the royal palace connected with it, the Pharaoh's offering to the god of abundant supplies of food, foreign revenues and a mercantile fleet, with many other donations appended in a meticulously detailed 'list of things, cattle, gardens, lands, galleys, workshops, and towns'. The concluding prayer of Ramesses to Amun for the success of his son specifies precisely those things which Solomon (according to the deuteronomic historian) was too virtuous to request:

Thou art the one who didst designate him to be king, while he was a youth. . . . Give to him a reign of millions of years. . . . Put his sword and his war-mace over the heads of the Bedouin; may they fall down in fear of him like Baal. Extend for him the boundaries as far as he desires; may the lands and countries fear in terror of him. . . . Give great and rich Niles in his time, in order to supply his reign with plentiful food. Give to him the princes who have not known Egypt, with loads upon their backs for his august palace.[39]

25

Later sections of the Great Harris Papyrus proudly record the Pharaoh's appointment of a multitude of officials and the elaboration of his internal administration: 'I made Egypt into many classes, consisting of: butlers of the palace, great princes, numerous infantry, and chariotry, by the hundred-thousand . . . attendants by the ten-thousand; and serf-labourers of Egypt.'[40] Although the personal names of the office-holders are not listed here, as they are in Solomon's Annals, other Egyptian records of the period, like those of the Harim Conspiracy[41] and the expedition of Ramesses IV to the greywacke quarries of Hammamat,[42] illustrate that such detail was much favoured by the scribes of Pharaoh's court. Incidentally, the latter document, boasting that the Pharaoh was accompanied by no less than 8,368 men (civil and military officers, artificers and artists, quarrymen and stone-cutters, overseers, slaves and soldiers), affords an interesting parallel to the statement in the Annals that 'Solomon had also seventy thousand hauliers and eighty thousand quarrymen, apart from the three thousand three hundred foremen in charge of the work who superintended the labourers. By the king's orders they quarried huge, massive blocks for laying the foundation of the Lord's house in hewn stone.'[43]

The Jerusalem temple dominates the Annals of Solomon, just as the temples of Medinet Habu, Heliopolis and Memphis dominate the Annals of Ramesses III in the Great Harris Papyrus. The biblical and Egyptian records agree in describing first the construction of the building and then a miscellany of accessory cultic equipment, although Solomon's scribes betray the novelty of their master's enterprise by a naïve delight in the details of its construction and ornamentation which is absent from the descriptions in the Egyptian documents.[44] They share, nevertheless, a vulgar emphasis on one-upmanship and on quantity and cost as the twin criteria of excellence. Thus we read in the Annals: 'Solomon put all these objects in their places; so great was the quantity of bronze used in their making that the weight of it was beyond all reckoning.'[45] Of the great throne of ivory,

Fig. 1   Painting from the Theban tomb of a Royal
Scribe (Dynasty XVIII). The detail is a part of the
decoration of a platform on which Amenophis III
sits enthroned, as foreigners, alternately negroes
and Syrians, make their submission.

it is reported, 'Nothing like it had ever been made for any
monarch';[46] and in general, it is claimed that 'the king made
silver as common in Jerusalem as stones.'[47] In a comparable
vein, the Great Harris Papyrus represents Ramesses III as
boasting: 'I filled its treasury with the products of the land of
Egypt: gold, silver, every costly stone by the hundred-
thousand. Its granary was overflowing with barley and
wheat; [its] lands, its herds, their multitudes were like the
sand of the shore.' Similarly, the Pharaoh's olives yield 'oil
more than the sand of the shore' and his herds 'were multiplied more than the sand'.[48] It is of no small interest to find
that this familiar Egyptian scribal cliché, natural to a people
constantly engaged in clearing sand after the inundation of
the Nile,[49] is used twice in the Annals – to describe the range
of Solomon's wisdom and the immense population of his
kingdom:

God gave Solomon depth of wisdom and insight, and understanding as wide as the sand on the sea-shore, so that Solomon's wisdom
surpassed that of all the men of the east and of all Egypt. . . . The
people of Judah and Israel were countless as the sands of the sea;
they ate and they drank, and enjoyed life. Solomon ruled over all
the kingdoms from the river Euphrates to Philistia and as far as the
frontier of Egypt; they paid tribute and were subject to him all
his life.[50]

That the occurrence of the cliché is more than merely coincidental is suggested by the scribes' boast that Solomon's unchallenged sovereignty enabled his people to enjoy the blessings of peace. This was a well-established feature in the eulogy of the Pharaohs and the Great Harris Papyrus follows the convention in claiming that perfect tranquillity prevailed under Ramesses III: 'Thou gavest peace and contentment of heart among my people, and every land was in adoration before me . . . I made the infantry and chariotry to dwell [at home] in my time. . . . Their bows and their weapons reposed in their magazines, while they were satisfied and drunk with joy.'[51]

SOLOMON – THE PHARAOH OF ISRAEL

If, as seems highly probable, the scribes of Solomon's court were deliberately adopting the literary conventions of their counterparts in Egypt, it is plausible to conclude that they were faithfully reflecting their royal master's policy of modelling his régime on that of the Pharaohs. Thus, Solomon's shipping enterprise on the Red Sea, which is the subject of a brief note in the Annals, follows an Egyptian precedent even older than the famous expedition of Queen Hatshepsut to Punt in the first half of the fifteenth century BC, and one which was still being maintained, as the Great Harris Papyrus records, in the reign of Ramesses III.[52]

Similarly, the diplomatic and commercial relations between Solomon and Hiram of Tyre are presented in a sparkling little narrative of which the substantial authenticity is confirmed rather than put into question when it is seen to be a miniature parallel to the famous Egyptian story of Wenamun's journey to Phoenicia in the reign of Ramesses XI (1113–1085 BC).[53] Wenamun, a Theban envoy despatched to Byblos to buy cedar wood for the sacred bark of Amon-Re, describes in this superbly vivid and humorous report how his mission was punctuated by robbery in Dor, ignominious delays in Byblos, and attempted murder in Cyprus. After protracted and humiliating negotiations, the Prince of Byblos eventually received what he regarded as adequate payment for the deal and 'fitted out 300 men and 300 oxen, and he placed superintendents in charge of them to cause them to fell the logs. And they felled them and they lay there during the winter. And in the third month of Summer they dragged them to the shore of the sea.'[54] So, just over a century later, the king of Tyre provided Solomon with timber for his temple: 'My men shall bring down the logs from Lebanon to the sea and I will make them up into rafts to be floated to the place you appoint.'[55]

The cordial relationship between Israel and Tyre, which allowed their rulers to negotiate the commercial agreement on more or less equal terms, contrasts significantly with the cold-shouldering of the Egyptian envoy by the Prince of Byblos. The unfortunate Wenamun was left in no doubt about his lack of credentials, credibility and credit:

'You shall pay me for doing it, and I will do it. Certainly my people performed this commission, but only after Pharaoh had caused to be brought six ships laden with Egyptian goods and they had unloaded them into their storehouses. But you – what have you brought to me myself?' And he caused the daybook rolls of his fathers to be brought and he caused them to be read before me. And they found entered on his roll a thousand *deben* of silver, things of all sorts. And he said to me: 'If the ruler of Egypt had been the possessor of mine own and I too his servant, he would not have caused silver and gold to be brought . . . it was no gratuitous gift that they used to make for my father. And as for me too, I myself, I am not your servant, and I am not the servant of him who sent you either.'[56]

Nothing could illustrate more clearly the nadir of Egypt's political prestige in the eleventh century BC and the power vacuum which had thus been created in the Ancient Near East.

If the petty kingdom of Byblos could begin to assert its independence of the former imperial power, how much greater were the opportunities for the emergent kingdom of Israel under David and Solomon. The Annals suggest that they were so avidly seized that the relationship of the record to Pharaonic models may be taken to indicate the imitation of Egypt's traditional imperial policy and not merely the imitation of the traditional literary style of its scribes.

CHAPTER TWO

The inheritance of Solomon

A PROFESSOR of modern history who recently declared that the really significant achievement of early Christianity was to break out of the 'tribal shell' of Judaism got his chronology wrong by almost exactly a thousand years. For it was in the first century of the first millennium B C, or, to be more precise, between 1000 and 930 B C, that Israel finally ceased to be anything like a 'tribal' society and emerged as a national state of great complexity and high pretensions, which, for a brief period, ranked as one of the major powers of the Ancient Near East. The phenomenal speed with which this revolution took place is unparalleled in antiquity and its final phases were accomplished only with the help of an articulate, highly professional, and ambitious bureaucracy.

It was begun, however, by a military genius who seized the opportunity provided by the momentous shift in the balance of power which marked the end of the second millennium B C in the area of the eastern Mediterranean. The Hittites and Egyptians, who for centuries had shared the rule of Syria-Palestine, were no longer factors to be reckoned with. About 1200 B C, the Hittite empire had completely succumbed to those enigmatic invading hordes from the west called by the Egyptians the 'Peoples of the Sea', and the growing weakness of Egypt after the death of Ramesses III had culminated in its collapse under the Twenty-first Dynasty (1085–935 B C). Although Assyria had started its military expansion towards the west as early as the end of the twelfth century B C, it had been unable to sustain it and was to remain of no account in the Fertile Crescent until the ninth century B C.

Fig. 2 Relief from the temple of Ramesses III at Medinet Habu (Dynasty XX). Four Egyptian ships (three at left and one at bottom right) are shown in action against three Philistine ships and two ships of their allies, the 'Peoples of the Sea'. The Egyptian ships are crescent-shaped and powered by both sail and oarsmen; their prow is decorated with the figure of a lioness devouring an Asiatic. The ships of the Philistines and their allies depend on sail alone and have a high stern and prow, the latter being designed as a duck's-bill battering weapon. The Philistines wear plumed helmets and their allies horned helmets. The scene shows the enemy ships trapped between the Egyptian fleet and the Egyptian archers ashore (extreme right).

This inviting power vacuum had already been entered by new aspirants to political and economic leadership – the Neo-Hittite kingdoms in northern Syria, the Aramean states in southern Syria and Transjordania, and the Philistines in Palestine. It was in this fluid situation that David, who came to the Israelite throne as the first millennium was beginning, saw the possibility of inaugurating a new era for his people. What he achieved may be measured by the Jerusalem scribes' proud statement of his successor's inheritance: 'Solomon ruled over all the kingdoms from the river Euphrates to Philistia and as far as the frontier of Egypt.'[1]

THE ARAMEANS
The extension of Israel's territory in the north-east as far as the Euphrates was, perhaps, David's boldest piece of empire-building. It marked his victory over the kingdom of Aram-Zobah, a formidable military power in southern Syria, which ruled the vast area bordered by Ammon in the south, the Syrian desert in the east and the Phoenician coastal region in the west. The defeat of Hadadezer, king of Aram-Zobah, brought Israel cheek by jowl with the Neo-Hittite kingdom of Hamath, whose ruler lost no time in ingratiating himself with the conqueror and even, perhaps, acknowledged David's suzerainty.[2] The significance of this subjugation of the Arameans is that it gave Israel control over the northern section of the Transjordanian caravan route from South Arabia to Mesopotamia known as the 'King's Highway', the southern section of which David secured by reducing the kingdoms of Ammon, Moab and Edom to vassal status.[3]

THE PHILISTINES
Control of the other and even more important trade route, the *Via Maris*, which ran up the coast from the Egyptian border, depended, in part, on the Philistines and Phoenicians. With Tyre, now the leading Phoenician city-state, David, like Solomon later, enjoyed good (and, presumably, mutually profitable) relations: 'Hiram king of Tyre,' we are told, 'sent an embassy to David; he sent cedar logs, and with them carpenters and stonemasons, who built David a house.'[4]

David's dealings with the Philistines, however, were far more tortuous. Having originally come to Saul's court as a professional soldier and won renown for the success of his mercenary troops in engagements with the Philistines, David was compelled, after his breach with the king, to take refuge in the Judean hills. Here, he became the leader of a band of desperadoes and 'drop-outs': 'Men in any kind of distress or in debt or with a grievance gathered round him, about four hundred in number, and he became their chief.'⁵ After aimlessly roaming the countryside, he finally sold his services (with a foreign legion now consisting of 600 men) to Achish, king of the Philistine city of Gath, who assigned to him the small city-state of Ziklag. This he appears to have used as a base for profitable looting exploits in the southern desert region and propagandist activities among its Judean population. It was only at the eleventh hour that David was spared the horror of fighting for his Philistine overlord against his own kith and kin at the decisive battle of Mount Gilboa, in which Saul and three of his sons (including Jonathan) lost their lives.⁶ The Philistines' military superiority, which, in the first place, had been largely responsible for galvanizing Israel into taking the momentous step of becoming a monarchy, now, ironically, brought the crown within the grasp of one of their own mercenaries.

During the seven and a half years of David's rule as king of Judah at Hebron, the Philistines were apparently content to regard him as a loyal vassal, but when, on Ishbaal's death, he also became king of Israel and moved his capital from Hebron to Jerusalem, they realized that a threatening change had taken place in the balance of power and so mounted two major assaults on the old Jebusite fortress. In these crucial engagements, their supremacy in Palestine was effectively and finally broken.⁷ David's defeat of the Philistines and their confinement to the coastal strip occupied by their confederation of city-states gave him mastery of the *Via Maris*.

THE ISRAELITE STATE

Israel's subjection to the Philistines was brought to an end by the Philistines' subjection to Israel and this meant, in effect, that the old Egyptian province of Palestine, which the Philistines had annexed in the twelfth century BC and ruled for 150 years, passed *en bloc* into David's hands. It also meant that the Canaanite system of city-states, which had survived for so long in vassalage, first to the Pharaoh and later to the

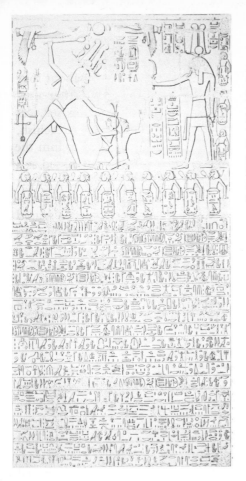

5 Inscription on the exterior of the temple of Ramesses III at Medinet Habu (Dynasty XX). It gives an address by Ptah to Ramesses III, in which the god promises the king a long and prosperous reign. In the scene above the inscription, Ramesses III sacrifices northern and southern captives to Ptah.

6 Sheet 79 of the Great Harris Papyrus (height 42 cm.) written *c.* 1166 BC in the reign of Ramesses IV (Dynasty XX).

7   One of the series of reliefs from Hatshepsut's temple at Deir el Bahari depicting her expedition to Punt (Dynasty XVIII). The Egyptians have almost completed the loading of their ships with a cargo which includes bags of incense and gold, ebony, ivory, skins of panthers, monkeys and frankincense trees. The elaborate precision and detail of these reliefs 'indicate an intense preoccupation with the natural world and an almost scientific eagerness to render the subject with as much authenticity as possible'. (Woldering, *The Arts of Egypt*).

8   Relief from the temple of Ramesses III at Medinet Habu (Dynasty XX). Ramesses III sacrifices captives of various racial types before the god Re-Harakhty, who extends to him the sickle-sword.

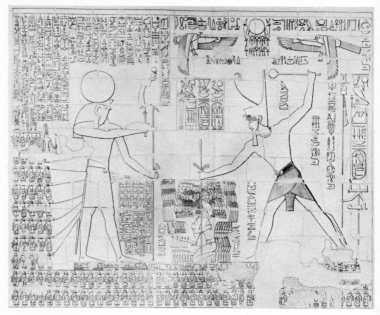

Philistines, was now finally integrated (as David's census for military service indicates[8]) into the structure of the new Israelite State. Jerusalem, it has been argued, was the one city-state in the country which was allowed to retain its ancient independent status, with David as the direct successor, in a personal and private capacity, of the previous Jebusite kings. This exceptional arrangement, which would have made David the ruler of *three* kingdoms – Israel, Judah *and* Jerusalem – has been interpreted as an astute move to insinuate dynastic monarchy into the Israelite system, as well as to establish a capital in neutral territory between the northern and southern kingdoms. The evidence for this is less conclusive than its wide acceptance might suggest and, in so far as it depends on the further hypothesis that the Israelite concept of monarchy was not dynastic, but 'charismatic' (a term strangely used by theologians to represent usurpers as divinely-chosen), there are reasons for rejecting it.[9]

Whether Israel's adoption of dynastic kingship 'like all the nations' is considered lamentable, admirable, or merely inevitable, it is clearly a fact that Saul was succeeded by his son Ishbaal, who (until he was murdered by his erstwhile protector) ruled 'all Israel', and that Solomon was designated king by David himself:

Take the officers of the household with you; mount my son Solomon on the king's mule and escort him down to Gihon. There Zadok the priest and Nathan the prophet shall anoint him king over Israel. Sound the trumpet and shout, 'Long live King Solomon!' Then escort him home again, and he shall come and sit on my throne and reign in my place; for he is the man that I have appointed prince over Israel and Judah.[10]

Documentary evidence like this, dating from the middle of the tenth century B C, suggests that Solomon inherited from David a concept of monarchy which was not only dynastic but already institutionalized.

THE LORD'S ANOINTED
The rite of anointing, which (perhaps anachronistically) is

37

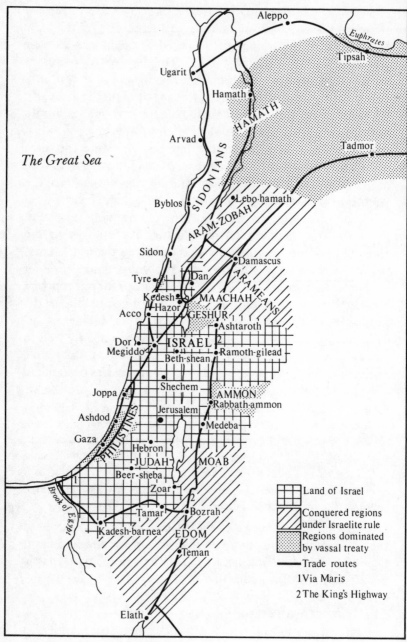

Fig. 3   The Kingdom of David.

represented as beginning with Saul, was the essential feature of the Israelite coronation ceremony and a cautious scholar has recently argued that it was an adaptation of the Egyptian practice of anointing vassal kings and the principal officers of the Pharaoh.[11] It is conceivable that the symbol had survived in the Canaanite tradition of Jerusalem. In becoming the Pharaoh's vassal, the king was assured of protection in return for his fidelity; so, it is suggested, the Davidic kings, as 'the Lord's anointed', were regarded as God's vassals and earthly representatives.

Later, in the ninth century B C, at the coronation of the boy king Joash, the rite of anointing is associated with the receiving of a document in which, it may be supposed, the terms of the vassal relationship were specified: 'Then he brought out the king's son, put the crown on his head, handed him the warrant and anointed him king.'[12] Whether or not such a 'warrant' or 'decree' was introduced into the coronation rite as early as the reign of David, and from which source it was borrowed, are controversial questions, more especially because they are intimately connected with the problematic dating and interpretation of evidence in the 'royal' psalms. The second psalm, for example, explicitly quotes the terms of the royal 'decree':

> I will repeat the Lord's decree:
> 'You are my son,' he said;
> 'this day I become your father.
> Ask of me what you will:
> I will give you nations as your inheritance,
> the ends of the earth as your possession.'

In this 'decree', all the emphasis falls on the privilege of the king's divine sonship and his sovereignty over the nations. In an academic area so heavily mined and so long fought over as that of Sacral Kingship in Ancient Israel, the prudent move with caution, but it is hardly possible to deny that many of the scribes who composed the royal psalms were drawing on concepts which, to say the least, had long been commonplace in Egypt. For centuries, the divine sonship of the Pharaoh had been upheld in myth and ritual and his sovereignty over the nations depicted in temple reliefs. To the brutality of these reliefs, the claim to universal dominion in the royal psalms often bears only too clearly an unhappy resemblance:

> Thou hast given me the shield of thy salvation,
> thy hand sustains me, thy providence makes me great . . .
> I pursue my enemies and overtake them,
> I do not return until I have made an end of them.
> I strike them down and they will never rise again;
> they fall beneath my feet . . .
> Thou settest my foot on my enemies' necks,
> and I bring to nothing those that hate me . . .
> I will pound them fine as dust before the wind,
> like mud in the streets will I trample them.
> Thou dost deliver me from the clamour of the people,
> and makest me master of the nations.[13]

The Egyptian motifs in many of the psalms seem unmistakable, but exactly when and how this element of the ancient culture of the Nile began to permeate the Israelite monarchy, it is impossible to judge with any degree of confidence.

THE NEW ORDER

There is no doubt, however, that David must be given the credit (if credit it be) of laying the foundations of Solomon's elaborate bureaucracy, as may be seen from the lists of their principal officers (to be discussed in the next chapter).[14] In David's list, it is not surprising to find that Joab, his army commander, is given pride of place and that, in contrast to Solomon's administration, the 'War Office' is allowed two representatives. Saul had already broken with hallowed Israelite tradition by establishing a corps of mercenaries in imitation of his Philistine enemies and it was, of course, as a professional soldier that David first came to his court. His appointment of Benaiah as commander of the 'Kerethite and Pelethite guards', who were foreign mercenaries (originally, perhaps, from Crete[15]) and quite distinct from the national

Israelite levy, indicates a further development of Saul's tentative innovation. Considering the scope of David's military enterprise, it is extraordinary that he never professionalized his army to the point of introducing chariotry.[16]

Nevertheless, it was David's massive achievement which made Solomon's chariotry possible, and there can be little doubt that it was he who made the decisive break with the old order of Israel. He created a national state, consolidated a dynastic monarchy, developed a professional army and, by the absorption of the Canaanite enclaves, vastly increased the number and cultural diversity of his subjects.

ISRAEL AND JUDAH

This monumental legacy was marred, however, by one major structural defect, which, had it not been for the efficiency of Solomon's absolutist government, would have brought about earlier the disruption which occurred at his death. The state which Solomon inherited was a *Personal-union*, that is, a combination of two independent political units (the later kingdoms of Israel and Judah) joined in the person of a single king, rather than a constitutionally united kingdom. Such 'personal unions' were not uncommon in the Ancient Near East, the most famous being that of Upper and Lower Egypt, and in the first years of the Hebrew monarchy this unsatisfactory political structure would, in any case, have been difficult to avoid.

The division between north and south was deep-seated. On the basis of an ancient list of tribal boundaries, which was later embedded in the book of Joshua, it has been suggested that in the period of the Judges (1200–1020 BC) the northern tribes (Ephraim, Manasseh, Benjamin, Zebulun, Asher and Naphtali) had formed themselves into a distinct and close-knit alliance, from which Judah was excluded.[17] The hypothesis receives a certain measure of support from the Song of Deborah, an indubitably ancient composition from about 1100 BC preserved as the fifth chapter of the book of Judges, since here the tribes which are praised for turning out to fight correspond to the 'northern alliance' and Judah is not mentioned.

If, then, as appears highly probably, David inherited a long-standing alienation between the population of the north and south, it was dangerous to risk exacerbating the situation by establishing his rule in two stages – first becoming 'king in Hebron over the house of Judah', and not until seven and a half years later, king 'over Israel and Judah together'. The dual character of David's régime is frequently noted in the biblical record and in the conduct of his deeply-resented military census it is explicitly acknowledged: 'Joab reported to the king the total number of people: the number of able-bodied men, capable of bearing arms, was 800,000 in *Israel* and 500,000 in *Judah*'.[18]

The latent antagonism between David's two kingdoms is, perhaps, best illustrated by the story-teller's lively recreation of the situation after the failure of Absalom's rebellion:

The men of Israel came to the king in a body and said, 'Why should our brothers of Judah have got possession of the king's person by joining King David's own men and then escorting him and his household across the Jordan?' The men of Judah replied, 'Because his majesty is our near kinsman. Why should you resent it? Have we eaten at the king's expense? Have we received any gifts?' The men of Israel answered, 'We have ten times your interest in the king and, what is more, we are senior to you; why do you disparage us? Were we not the first to speak of bringing the king back?' The men of Judah used language even fiercer than the men of Israel.[19]

The same gifted writer highlights the danger inherent in this cleavage by recording, as the immediate sequel, Sheba's incitement of the north to revolt:

> What share have we in David?
> We have no lot in the son of Jesse.
> Away to your homes, O Israel.

This was the watchword two generations later when, after

Solomon's death, Israel rejected his son for a king of their own choosing.[20]

If by moving his capital to the no-man's-land of Jerusalem and by installing the Ark there, David supposed that he would be able to unite the factions of north and south and provide a rallying-point for conservative Israelite opinion, his hopes were largely disappointed. The disruption of the dual monarchy as soon as Solomon's tight control was relaxed provides incontrovertible evidence of its chronic instability.

MONARCHY AND THEOCRACY

The extent of David's achievement in transforming Israel into a theocratic state is much more difficult to measure, since the sources leave room for more than one view of the 'tribal' character of pre-monarchical Israel and, in consequence, for more than one assessment of the size of David's task in establishing the new polity.

The reconstruction of the life and history of pre-monarchical Israel has always afforded a field day for the exercise of unacknowledged presuppositions. Apart from the crypto-fundamentalism of those who exploit archaeology to prove that the Bible is *nearly* true, these presuppositions largely concern the genesis and significance of political institutions. For example, the most popular presupposition about the genesis of the monarchy used to be that it is evolution which provides the appropriate model and enables the historian to trace Israel's steady progress in settling down – from nomadic tribe to national state. Such confidence in the superior value of the end-product harmonizes easily with the quite different presupposition that theocracy, in any case, demands a human institution invested with divine authority. Those who hold the latter dogma are not, however, committed to an evolutionary model for the genesis of the Israelite monarchy, but may equally take the view that in the beginning a religious community was created *ab extra*, of

43

which the monarchy faithfully perpetuated the fundamental structure. Thus, presuppositions about what is inevitable and what is desirable determine our view about what actually happened. The current academic fashion in these matters is to emphasize not only the origin of Israel as a community created by a common faith, but also its structured religio-political character as a tribal league or 'amphictyony', with a central (but changeable) sanctuary, regular festivals, and even established officials, like the so-called 'minor judges'.[21] If this view of pre-monarchical Israel is well founded, David's task of inaugurating a 'divine state' based on a dynasty of 'sacral kings' cannot – such was the continuity – have been unduly burdensome.

The complex of presuppositions by which this widely-accepted reconstruction is shaped has now been vigorously challenged on the basis of a totally different and, at first glance, dubiously 'modern' model.[22] The Hebrews in the second millennium BC, it is argued, are to be seen not as semi-nomadic tribesmen but as discontented 'drop-outs'. They were rebels who had rejected the royal and religious civilization of the Canaanite city-states and opted out of urban society. That this model is not simply a crass twentieth-century anachronism may be seen by relating it to a category of persons called *'Apiru*, who are mentioned in all the archives so far discovered in the Ancient Near East from the second millennium BC. According to a recent study, the *'Apiru* 'would seem to have been composed of uprooted, propertyless persons who found a means of subsistence for themselves and their families by entering a state of dependence'. They 'were an element of the settled rather than of the desert or nomadic population' and, so far from being a closed ethnic group, they attracted 'all sorts of fugitive and footloose persons who were impelled by misdeed or misfortune to leave their homes'. There are difficulties in the way of making any simple equation between *'Apiru* and Hebrew, but it is by no means impossible that 'the beginnings of Israelite history were bound up with a "wandering

Fig. 4   Line drawing of an ivory plaque (length 26 cm) from Megiddo (14th–12th century BC). A king is celebrating a military victory from a throne flanked by two sphinxes. It has been suggested that the figure in the chariot is another representation of the king himself. The winged solar-disc (on the right) is Asian and the long garments Syrian in type, although the basic artistic convention is Egyptian.

Aramean" whose social status and mode of life mark him as an *'Apiru*.'[23]

It is, therefore, worth pausing over the suggestion that what happened between Moses and the monarchy was less an *invasion* of nomadic tribes from some unidentified region beyond the borders of Palestine than an *uprising* of those members of the settled population who were 'suffering under the burden of subjection to a monopoly of power which they had no part in creating, and from which they received virtually nothing but tax-collectors'.[24] On this hypothesis, such discontented 'Hebrews' became 'Israelites' at the moment when they chose to throw in their lot with that small invading group, once slaves in Egypt and, like them, stateless persons, who under the leadership of Moses had been drawn into a new religious community – Israel, the people of God. If, in fact, pre-monarchical Israel discovered its identity and solidarity as a new religious community, which had opted out of the royal and religious society of Late Bronze Age Canaan, David's success in establishing even a modified version of the all-too-familiar sacral state can have been achieved only in the teeth of the most vehement opposition.

Such opposition may be detected in the revolt of that 'scoundrel named Sheba', and in the literary stratum of the biblical record which describes the original institution of the

45

monarchy as an outright rejection of the rule of God.[25] It appears also in the so-called 'dynastic oracle' of the second book of Samuel and accounts for the fact that this is so highly ambivalent a statement. It seems clear, however, that the late writer of this passage was fully aware of the difficulty of reconciling the new royal régime of David with Israel's ancestral faith:

As soon as the king was established in his house and the Lord had given him security from his enemies on all sides, he said to Nathan the prophet, 'Here I live in a house of cedar, while the Ark of God is housed in curtains.' Nathan answered the king, 'Very well, do whatever you have in mind, for the Lord is with you.' But that night the word of the Lord came to Nathan. . . . 'Are you the man to build me a house to dwell in? Down to this day I have never dwelt in a house since I brought Israel up from Egypt.'

Here Nathan speaks for those who believed that David's installation of the Ark in Jerusalem was at best a confidence trick and at worst a sell-out. He had built for himself a 'house of cedar' in imitation of Canaanite kings and it followed with devastating inevitability (as Solomon proved) that God himself would be drawn into this alien royal milieu and similarly localized in a 'house of cedar' in imitation of Canaanite deities.[26] Stephen, the first Christian martyr, made an acute historical judgment when he interpreted the establishment of the monarchy as provoking the first major crisis of Israel's history, but, in apportioning the responsibility for it, he was probably unaware of the Canaanite character of Solomon's inheritance: 'David found favour with God and asked to be allowed to provide a dwelling-place for the God of Jacob; but it was Solomon who built him a house. However, the Most High does not live in houses made by men.'[27] It was, we may surmise, only David's lack of opportunity which saved his reputation for orthodoxy.

CHAPTER THREE

The new bureaucracy

SIGNIFICANTLY, it is only for the reigns of David and Solomon that the Old Testament provides a formal list of State Officials.[1] Much scholarly ingenuity has been expended on the translation of their Hebrew titles, although a few moments' reflection on the English offices of 'Speaker' and 'Home Secretary' (not to mention those members of the Royal Household entitled the 'Clerk of the Closet' and the 'Ladies of the Bedchamber') will suggest that what an official is called may throw very little light of what he actually does. Unfortunately, the functions of Solomon's principal officials are never described fully enough to give a firm lead to the translator, and so he is forced to depend a good deal (despite the protests of learned students of etymology) on general judgment and plausible historical analogues.

THE SECRETARY OF STATE
The list for David's reign poses the first problem and, in doing so, yields the first clue of major significance. Seraiah, it is said, was David's *sopher*;[2] a second version of the list gives the office to Sheva;[3] and in the list for Solomon's reign, he reappears with the name Shisha.[4] It has recently been demonstrated that *Sheva* and *Shisha* are corruptions not of the proper name Seraiah but of the title of his office *in its original Egyptian form*.[5] The Egyptian term means 'letter-writer', which corresponds to the Hebrew title *sopher*, often translated in the Old Testament as 'secretary' or 'scribe'.[6] However, the acceptance of an Egyptian background to the office of *sopher*, so far from clarifying its functions and status, serves

only to increase its ambiguity, since in the Pharaoh's administration *all* civil servants, from the highest officials to the lowliest clerks, were called 'scribes', just as in England 'secretary' covers the whole range from Her Majesty's Secretary of State for Foreign Affairs to the clerks who act as secretaries to the Secretary to the Private Secretary to the Queen.

A plausible restoration of the order of the list for David's reign[7] makes the Secretary, as in Solomon's list,[8] the first civil official of the kingdom and some such rank is supported by the seniority of later holders of the title in Judah. Among these, Shaphan, at the end of the seventh century B C, was the head of a family with a particularly distinguished record of public service.[9] The Old Testament, unfortunately, is far from illuminating about the duties of the Secretary, and when he is discovered engaged in trivial chores as temple treasurer in the reign of Joash (837–800 B C),[10] it is necessary to remember that the kingdom at that point was on the verge of collapse and that, in any case, the history of Judah after Solomon's reign is, for the most part, a record of rapid decline. The title 'royal scribe', however, was held by many high-ranking officials in Egypt and the 'royal letter-scribe of Pharaoh' occupied a key position in the kingdom. There can be little doubt, therefore, that it was from this home of bureaucracy (whether directly or indirectly) that David borrowed the model for the leading member of his new civil administration and that, with the increased responsibilities of the office under Solomon, its holder fully merits the title of Secretary of State.[11]

THE ROYAL HERALD

Next in order on David and Solomon's lists, and closely associated with the Secretary of State in critical diplomatic negotiations two hundred years later, we find the Royal Herald. The Hebrew title *mazkir*, meaning one who calls, proclaims, names, reminds and reports, corresponds exactly with the Egyptian title of a high-ranking civil servant who acted as intermediary between the Pharaoh and his people. He combined, it seems, the roles of *éminence grise*, Lord Chamberlain, Aide-de-Camp, Public Relations Officer and Spokesman for the Palace, all of which, it must be admitted, the conventional translation 'Royal Herald' is under some strain to convey.[12]

THE STEWARD

The triumvirate of principal civil officials is completed by the Steward, whose title ('over the house') appears for the first time in Solomon's administration. The high status of this office in the later years of the Judean kingdom is suggested by the fact that it was held by no less a person than Jotham, son of Uzziah, during his period as regent. Its dignity is confirmed by the terms in which Isaiah announced the dismissal of the self-seeking Shebna, Steward of Hezekiah (715–687 BC):

On that day I will send for my servant Eliakim son of Hilkiah; I will invest him with your robe, gird him with your sash; and hand over your authority to him. He shall be a father to the inhabitants of Jerusalem and the people of Judah. I will lay the key of the house of David on his shoulder; what he opens no man shall shut, and what he shuts no man shall open.

It has been noted that one of the many duties of the Egyptian Vizier was similarly described, for example, in the tomb inscriptions of Rekhmire, who held office under Tuthmosis III: 'the vizier shall send to open every gate of the king's-house, to cause to go in all that goes in, [and] to go out all that goes out.'[13] There can be little doubt that the prophet's language reflects a daily administrative procedure ultimately derived from the Egyptian court, but this is far from establishing, as some scholars hold, that Eliakim's office corresponded to that of the Vizier himself.[14] It is more probable that the Egyptian model being followed is that of the Chief Steward of the King, who was responsible for the vast personal estates of the Pharaoh, and from his favoured position in the palace wielded immense power – parallel to, but distinct from, that of the Vizier in the national administration.[15] Although in Solomon's list the Steward occupies a very modest position, it is probable that his office was already more far-reaching than the title 'Comptroller of the household' (adopted by the New English Bible) suggests and that, in addition to supervising the domestic arrangements of the palace, it included the management of the king's private estates.

CROWN PROPERTY AND PATRONAGE

The sharp distinction between the property of the state and the personal property of the king, which was recognized in Egypt, is less easy to establish for the kingdom of Solomon, but it is virtually certain that, in addition to the royal estates inherited directly from Saul and David, Solomon assumed ownership of much of the territory which had recently been annexed from the Canaanite regions.[16] It was presumably in these less conservative and controversial districts that the king farmed his own estates and assigned land in fee to courtiers, bureaucrats and others whose loyalty and services had to be paid for.[17] It is even conceivable that Solomon followed the notorious Egyptian precedent of assigning royal lands to the temple priesthood, if, indeed, the roster of forty-eight levitical cities presupposed by the lists in the book of Joshua and the first book of Chronicles did, as is widely thought, originate as early as his reign and record the settlement of Levites in the border territories acquired from the Canaanites.[18]

At least we may be confident that one of Solomon's first acts as king was to dismiss Abiathar from the priesthood and assign him a royal estate, so that the more amenable Zadok might be installed in his place. Significantly, it is a son of Zadok who heads the administrative list of this temple-building potentate.[19] It may safely be surmised that Solomon's ecclesiastical policy reflected the Egyptian tradition of his senior civil servants, in which it was taken for granted that priests were as much the Pharaoh's agents as any other members of his administration and equally subject to his power of appointment and dismissal.

ADMINISTRATIVE DISTRICTS

Solomon's personal estate, we may take it, made some small contribution towards the 'thirty kor [?5 tons] of flour and sixty kor [?10 tons] of meal, ten fat oxen and twenty oxen from the pastures and a hundred sheep, as well as stags, gazelles, roebucks, and fattened fowl',[20] which, the scribe claims, were consumed daily at the palace, but the annual budget for the court, military establishment, civil service and public works clearly demanded a much more systematic exploitation of the nation's resources. The king's bureaucrats were equal to the situation and simply adopted a system of taxation which had proved efficient in Egypt.

The country was divided into twelve administrative districts, each under the control of a governor, who, according to the record, was responsible for providing one month's supply of food a year 'for the king and the royal household'.[21] It has been suggested that the districts were defined with a view to creating units of approximately equal economic capacity,[22] but, considering the diversity of the land, even office-bound bureaucrats are unlikely to have entertained so unrealistic a concept and, if they did, the disparity, for example, between the fertile district of Megiddo and the impoverished district of Benjamin must have given rise to difficulties. Economic parity would obviously have been desirable if each district was, in fact, intended to feed the court for 'a month in turn' each year, but (despite the Egyptian precedent) this seems highly improbable. However, beneath the naiveté of the official presentation – *ad maiorem gloriam Solomonis* – it is possible to discern in the plan a solid substratum of political and economic realism.

Politically, it was necessary to secure the precarious unity of the state, constantly threatened by David's burdensome legacy of a dual monarchy, in which Israel and Judah were

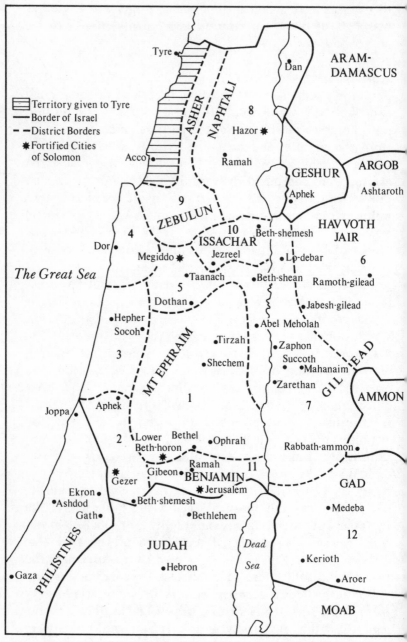

Fig. 5 Solomon's administrative districts and fortified cities.

held together by the frail *Personal union* of a common king, and weakened by the absorption of new and as yet non-aligned Canaanite territories alien to the old tribal structure.[23] Solomon's scheme of twelve districts implemented an unprecedented policy of centralization by which Jerusalem became the administrative hub of the kingdom. Whatever David thought, the filing cabinets of the capital, it was judged, were more likely to pull things together than the Ark of the Covenant. It would have been possible for Solomon's men to have acted as new brooms in a clean sweep of the traditional social order (as happened in France when departments were created to break up local loyalties), but their definition of the twelve districts suggests no such foolish intention. Four of them were named after tribes – Naphtali, Asher, Issachar, Benjamin – and a fifth (Mahanaim), though identified by the name of a city, was equally a continuation of a traditional Israelite settlement. The central district in 'the hill-country of Ephraim' did, however, represent a radical departure from the past, in that its western boundary excluded part of the tribal inheritance of Manasseh and forced it into an administrative relationship with the new Canaanite area on the Sharon Plain. This arrangement may well have been a deliberate political move to weaken the powerful northern combination of Ephraim and Manasseh (the so-called 'house of Joseph'), which had probably already made a bid for the leadership of the former Canaanite territories. These were now organized into five separate districts, administered from Jerusalem, and so detached from the political intrigues of the north.[24]

DISTRICT GOVERNORS

Political acumen may also be traced in the appointments which were made to these new and manifestly important district governorships. The list includes two sons-in-law of the king, of whom one, Ahimaaz, was probably the son of Zadok, and, therefore, brother of the priest at the head of Solomon's administration; Baana, 'son of Ahilud', looks like the brother of the Royal Herald and it is a plausible guess that Baanah, 'son of Hushai', was the child of David's trusted counsellor.[25] This nepotism may simply follow a not unfamiliar Near Eastern custom, but it is conceivable that it reflects the paramount importance of Solomon's having safe men in strategic positions. It would be good to know whether any significance should be attached to the fact that five of the district governors are listed without their first names, only the patronymic being used. The generally-accepted view that damage to the upper right-hand margin of the list erased the first names of these men has to reckon with the fact that the fifth has been preserved but not the sixth, and, more seriously, with the recent recognition that the use of the patronymic alone was established Canaanite practice for families in the King's Service. It is possible, therefore, that Ben-hur, Ben-dekar, Ben-hesed, Ben-abinadab and Ben-geber, of whom the last four governed new Canaanite districts, were men of good standing in the local community, whom Solomon astutely took over for his own administration. Such a policy would, at least, have been in line with his appointment (in a much more sensitive sphere) of Zadok, who was probably formerly a priest of the Canaanite sanctuary of Jerusalem, which may have continued to function after David captured the city.[26]

The final verse of the list of district governors is, unfortunately, obscure and textually suspect. The point of substance is whether the 'one governor in the land' refers to Judah and, if not, whether Judah may be regarded, nevertheless, as included in the new administrative system. Scholarship runs true to form in producing on this issue a weight of comment inversely proportional to the weight of the available evidence. On general grounds, however, it seems highly improbable that Solomon would have so far undermined his fundamental objective of creating 'one nation' as blatantly to exempt the southern kingdom and, to add insult to injury, by a scheme which was administered from the Office of the Superintendent of the Regional

Governors, comfortably ensconced in the tax-free area of Jerusalem.[27]

TAXATION

The details of Solomon's system of taxation his scribes judged it prudent to keep dark and the only way of correcting their tendentious delicacy is to have recourse to that (no doubt equally tendentious) denunciation of the monarchy, which a later writer ascribed to the foresight of Samuel:

This will be the sort of king who will govern you. . . . He will take your sons and make them serve in his chariots and with his cavalry, and will make them run before his chariot. Some he will appoint officers over units of a thousand and units of fifty. Others will plough his fields and reap his harvest; others again will make weapons of war and equipment for mounted troops. He will take your daughters for perfumers, cooks, and confectioners, and will seize the best of your cornfields, vineyards, and olive-yards, and give them to his lackeys. He will take a tenth of your grain and your vintage to give to his eunuchs and lackeys. Your slaves, both men and women, and the best of your cattle and your asses he will seize and put to his own use. He will take a tenth of your flocks, and you yourselves will become his slaves.[28]

As unambiguously as the royal scribes, this ancestral voice of Israel is claiming that Solomon had modelled himself on the Pharaohs of Egypt; the two sides of the coin fit exactly.

In Egypt, during the New Kingdom (1567–1065 BC), it was the mayors of the principal towns who acted as provincial officials and their chief function was collecting the taxes in kind levied upon their districts, for which they were directly answerable to the Vizier's office in the capital.[29] Such, we may be confident, was the chief function of Solomon's district governors.

THE CORPS OF CHARIOTRY

The scribes boast and Samuel laments that the people bore the burden of one of Solomon's most spectacular and expensive

55

innovations – the corps of chariotry.[30] It was during the period of Hyksos rule in the Delta that the Egyptians learnt how to use the light war-chariot and it is first represented on a scarab of Tuthmosis I (1525–1512 BC).[31] About the same time, chariotry reached Crete and the mainland of Greece and rapidly became the indispensable arm throughout Mesopotamia and Syria. The Israelites had, indeed, encountered the weapon in their struggles with the Canaanites and Philistines, but they were so far out of touch with international developments that even as late as the reign of David chariot-horses captured in battle were simply hamstrung.[32] Solomon, the record proudly proclaims, changed all that and brought his kingdom up to date: 'he had fourteen hundred chariots and twelve thousand horses, and he stabled some in the chariot-towns and kept others at hand in Jerusalem.'[33]

Three of these chariot-towns have recently been excavated (Hazor, Megiddo, and Gezer) and although the stable complex discovered at Megiddo is now assigned to the period of Ahab (869–850 BC) its size, with space for about 150 chariots and 450 horses, is some indication, at least, that the claim of 1400 chariots for Solomon is not a ridiculous exaggeration. According to the Assyrian record, Ahab was able to muster a force of 2000 chariots at the battle of Qarqar in 853 BC. Solomon's chariots were imported, we are told, from Egypt at 600 silver shekels each.[34] The figure of 12,000 horses is more difficult to judge. It is generally agreed that neither Egypt nor Israel used cavalry, which first entered the Fertile Crescent with Assyria's mounted divisions in the ninth century BC,[35] and since riding appears to have been one of the few status symbols which Solomon failed to adopt from the Pharaohs,[36] all the king's horses would be for use in his chariots. With two in harness and one held in reserve, the minimum complement must have been well over 4000.

In Egypt, the corps of chariotry had its own internal administration staffed by scribes[37] and a comparable organization, if on a smaller scale, may be assumed as an inevitable consequence of Solomon's innovation. Whether, however, the king was interested in developing his army for purposes other than display and defence may well be doubted. The royal scribes made much of the peace enjoyed throughout his reign and Benaiah, the old leader of David's mercenary troops, was now in sole charge as Commander of the Army, with, it appears from the official lists, a loss of seniority.

FORCED LABOUR

A clue to the changed position may be found in Solomon's addition of another new post to his administration – the Superintendent of the Forced Levy,[38] part of whose business was to conscript as a labour force the men made redundant by the institution of a regular army: 'King Solomon raised a forced levy from the whole of Israel amounting to thirty thousand men. He sent them to Lebanon in monthly relays of ten thousand, so that the men spent one month in Lebanon and two at home; Adoniram was superintendent of the whole levy.'[39] The term 'levy' (*mas*) is derived from the Akkadian *massu*, meaning a conscripted labour gang, like that sent to cultivate Egyptian Crown property at Shunem, about which the king of Megiddo wrote one of the Amarna letters to the Pharaoh.[40] The *corvée*, as the institution is often called, involved temporary *ad hoc* service when there was a particular job to be done – in Solomon's case felling timber and quarrying stone for 'all his cherished plans for building in Jerusalem'. This ancient and common method of carrying out public works was so much a part of life in Egypt that it was expected to continue in the Hereafter and facsimiles were put in tombs to act as the dead man's stand-in, against the day when he was 'registered for work which is to be done in the Underworld as a man under obligation, to cultivate the fields, to irrigate the banks, to transport sand of the east and of the west.'[41] If the Egyptians were accustomed to the *corvée*, the Israelites were not, and they expressed their resentment by seizing Solomon's Superintendent and stoning him to death.[42] Ironically, it was one of Adoniram's underlings,

Figs. 6, 7   Painting from the Theban tomb of Rekhmire, Vizier under Tuthmosis III and Amenophis II (Dynasty XVIII). Fair-skinned, bearded Syrians and dark-skinned Nubians are represented among the slaves.

Jeroboam, at one time 'in charge of all the labour-gangs in the tribal district of Joseph', who, whether moved by a change of heart or mere opportunism, broke with Solomon, threw in his lot with the northern rebels and became the first ruler of the independent kingdom of Israel.[43] This evidence is too circumstantial to be contradicted by the pious assertion of a later editor that 'Solomon put none of the Israelites to forced labour; they were his fighting men', but a greater degree of credibility attaches to his claim that Solomon employed his Canaanite subjects, recently brought within the structure of the state, 'on *perpetual* forced labour' (*mas 'obed*).[44] For these wretches, there was no question of spending two months out of three at home, for state slavery, as an institution, did not recognize the existence of human rights.

Civil servants
State slavery is the darkest symbol of a régime which exercised absolute power. Solomon's principal officers – the First Priest, the Secretary of State, the Royal Herald, the Steward, the Superintendent of the Regional Governors, and the

Superintendent of the Forced Levy – should not be thought of as 'cabinet ministers'; on the contrary, they were simply civil servants – the agents of their master's sovereign will and the means by which he imposed his decisions on every department of the state and ultimately, through a bureaucratic hierarchy, on each one of his subjects. The confusing references in the Annals of Solomon to the 550 officers in charge of the 3,300 foremen who superintended the 70,000 hauliers and 80,000 quarrymen engaged on the King's Works are only hints that in grandeur and complexity of organization Solomon's state was run on classical Egyptian lines.[45] The Egyptian records are full of statistics about the different categories of workers employed on royal building sites and reveal the bureaucrat's obsession with meticulous detail. The scribes who supervised the tomb-builders of Thebes, for example, recorded not only the workers' absences and rations of grain, but even the number of lamp-wicks issued to men quarrying in the dark and the name and condition (fresh, dry or cut-up) of the regular deliveries of fish.[46] The same delight in lists and the complexities of administration is illustrated in a letter of the Ramesside period (1320–1085 BC) from 'the scribe Bekenptah' to 'the scribe Kawiser':

When my letter reaches you you shall cause the great dyke to be made. . . . Mark the multitude of subordinates you have here. To let you know everyone by his name. Catalogue of jobs of men, plebeians, and craftsmen; the totality of all performers of tasks who are capable. with their hands, performers of manual labour and office jobs, magistrates commanding administrators, chief major-domo, mayor, headmen of villages, quartermaster . . . chief of departments, scribe of the offering-table, controllers, retainer, messenger of administrators, brewer, baker, butcher, servant, confectioner, baker of . . . cakes, butler tasting the wine, chief of works, overseer of carpenters, chief-craftsman, deputy, draughts-man, sculptor, miner, quarryman, demolisher, stone-worker . . . barber, basket-maker.[47]

All these subordinates were under the supervision of scribes and it was just such a class of educated civil servants, for so many centuries the dominant influence in Egyptian society, that Solomon created in Israel.

CHAPTER FOUR

The king's works

THE WINDOW in King's College Chapel, Cambridge, which depicts the visit of the Queen of Sheba to King Solomon, shows the two separated by an area of blue glass. This curious feature reflects, like the web-footed queen of Chartres, the eccentric Islamic development of the biblical story, according to which Solomon, led to suspect that the queen is a hairy-legged seductress, tricks her into lifting her skirts by the ruse of a glass floor easily mistaken for a pool of water. No such unworthy suspicions are to be found in the alternative, Ethiopian, development of the original narrative. In this tradition, it is the king who seduces the virgin queen, and the son born of their union becomes the founder of the Ethiopian dynasty and heir to the divine promises made to the Davidic dynasty. Indeed, the 1955 Ethiopian Constitution (Article 2) endows the age-old legend with the status of law: 'the Imperial dignity shall remain perpetually attached to the line . . . [which] descends without interruption from the dynasty of Menelik I, son of the Queen of Ethiopia, the Queen of Sheba, and King Solomon of Jerusalem.' When this fantasy was first committed to writing early in the fourteenth century A D, its purpose, like that of the biblical Succession Story, was to uphold the claims of the recently established 'Solomonic' dynasty in Ethiopia. Of the two lines of development only the Ethiopian version preserves any hint of the basically commercial relationship which may be read between the lines of the original narrative. It recounts how the queen's visit to Jerusalem arose out of enthusiastic reports from her Controller of Caravans, who was already engaged in large-scale trading operations with Solomon.[1]

TRADE BY LAND AND SEA

Solomon in his assumed role of an oriental potentate, with 'courtiers sitting round him, and his attendants standing behind in their livery', had, no doubt, introduced to his court such South Arabian luxuries as frankincense and myrrh, but it is probable that his interest in spices was as much commercial as cosmetic. His Annals refer to the tolls levied by his customs officers and 'the tribute of the kings of Arabia'[2] and it is reasonable to deduce that it was principally about this aspect of Solomon's wisdom that the Queen of Sheba travelled 1,500 miles to ask him hard questions. After David had reduced Edom, Moab, Ammon, Aram-Zobah and Aram-Damascus to vassal status, and made a favourable treaty with Toi of Hamath, it was possible, as we have seen, for Solomon to exercise complete control of the 'King's Highway' – the vital caravan route, which ran from South Arabia along eastern Transjordan to Damascus and Mesopotamia.[3] That such control was a considerable national asset is clear both from the wars fought over it by the great powers of the Fertile Crescent ever since the third millennium BC, and from statistics supplied by Pliny a thousand years after Solomon's golden age of opportunity. In his *Natural History*, Pliny reports that by the time a caravan reached the Mediterranean, the cost per camel-load of frankincense, largely owing to custom tolls en route, amounted to no less than 688 *denarii*, which has been ingeniously calculated to mean that a pound of the spice cost (according to quality) the equivalent of a working man's wage for between a week and a fortnight.[4]

It was Solomon's recognition that the 'King's Highway' was of crucial importance to the national economy that led him to fortify both the northern outposts of Tadmor (later Palmyra),[5] a staging-post half-way between Damascus and the Euphrates, and Ezion-geber, the southern Red Sea port on the Gulf of Aqaba. Although the excavator of Ezion-geber withdrew his original claim that it was a major centre for the mining and refining of copper, he continued to ascribe

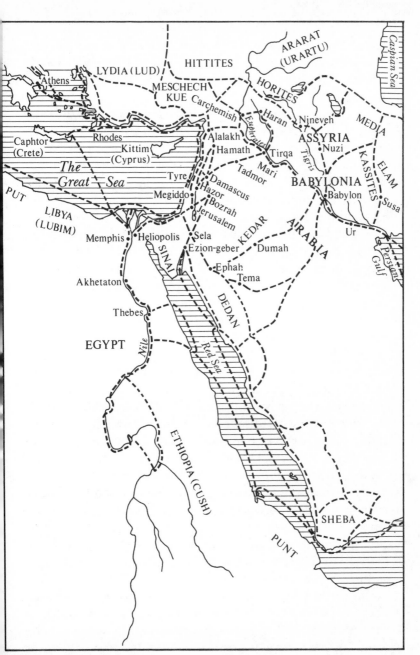

Fig. 8   The Ancient Near East and its trade routes.

to Solomon's initiative there a citadel-cum-storehouse protected by substantial casemate walls. This modest structure,
however, fails to reveal the significance of Ezion-geber as the
northern terminus for freighters plying the Red Sea coast
from the gum-resin centres of South Arabia and the northern
coast of Somaliland. This sea-route provided an alternative
to the first stages of the caravan trail north across the Arabian
peninsula, which, we may imagine, was easier for tribesmen
to exploit for protection money than for civil servants to
administer from Jerusalem. It was for this solid commercial
reason that Solomon collaborated with Hiram, king of Tyre,
in building and operating a merchant fleet.

Two of the three references to Solomon's fleet record that
it brought back gold from Ophir and the third reports that
'every three years this fleet of merchantmen came home,
bringing gold and silver, ivory, apes and monkeys.'[6] The
location of Ophir is still debated, although a Hebrew ostracon
recently found at Tell Qasileh (now within the city boundaries of Tel Aviv) and dated in the eighth century BC has at
last brought it to earth from the realm of legend: 'Gold of
Ophir for Beth-horon 30 shekels.'[7] Most scholars speculate
that Ophir was near the southern end of the Red Sea, either
in one of the prosperous regions of South Arabia or in
Somaliland. Recent discussion of the biblical language describing the imports from Ophir has removed 'peacocks'
from the traditional list and so weakened the arguments for
finding its location in India. It seems, however, that as early
as the fifteenth century BC, the Egyptian Queen Hatshepsut
obtained cinnamon, a product native to Ceylon, in Somaliland (Punt), and this is taken to suggest that Indian (and,
perhaps, Arab) merchantment were already bringing goods
from India to ports near the Red Sea, where they were trans-
shipped for local distribution. Also, we have it on Pliny's
authority that by the first century AD Graeco-Roman merchant fleets based in Egypt were making the round trip to
the west coast of India in little over a year. It would, therefore, be hazardous to deny too hastily, either that the

Phoenician merchant venturers of Solomon's time could have managed the Arabia–India route 'once every three years', or that the whereabouts of Ophir still remains an open question. It is even possible that Tyre actually demanded a lucrative outlet to the Indian Ocean in exchange for the considerable contribution it was making to Solomon's other state enterprises.[8]

Solomon's dependence on his alliance with Tyre is well illustrated by his cession to Hiram of 'twenty cities in the land of Galilee'. The tendentious biblical accounts of this transaction[9] attempt to gloss over or deny the seriousness of losing such a valuable thirty-mile stretch of Israelite coastal hinterland, which not only included the small harbour of Acco, but, much more important, controlled a vital section of the *Via Maris*. This, it will be recalled, was the grand alternative to the 'King's Highway' and provided the most direct route from Egypt to Mesopotamia. From the Egyptian border, the 'Way of the Sea' followed the coastline to the Plain of Sharon and after swinging inland to Megiddo forked into two major routes. The western branch ran along the Phoenician coast to northern Syria and Cilicia and the eastern branch through the plain of Jezreel to Hazor and Damascus, where it merged with the 'King's Highway' and its traffic for Mesopotamia.

It is obvious that the *Via Maris* was a vital land bridge to every Ancient Near Eastern nation with imperial or commercial ambitions, and the entertaining *Satirical Letter* by the scribe Hori shows how thoroughly it was studied in Egyptian schools during the thirteenth century BC. In addition to providing an invaluable gazetteer of place names, Hori sometimes shows off his literary flair in 'travelogue' descriptions, as when he traces the progress of a lonely charioteer through the hazardous pass connecting Megiddo and the Plain of Sharon:

The narrow valley is dangerous with Bedouin, hidden under the bushes. Some of them are of four or five cubits from their noses to the heel [seven to nine feet tall], and fierce of face. Their hearts are not mild, and they do not listen to wheedling. Thou art alone; there is no messenger with thee, no army host behind thee. . . . Thou comest to a decision by going forward, although thou knowest not the road. Shuddering seizes thee, the hair of thy head stands up, and thy soul lies in thy hand. Thy path is filled with boulders and pebbles . . . overgrown with reeds, thorns, brambles, and 'wolf's-paw'. The ravine is on one side of thee, and the mountain rises on the other. Thou goest on jolting, with thy chariot on its side, afraid to press thy horse too hard. . . . Thou startest to trot. The sky is opened [he comes out of the valley into the open]. Then thou thinkest that the foe is behind thee. . . . The horse is played out by the time thou findest a night-quarters.[10]

The harrowing experience of Hori's charioteer recalls that it was also along the *Via Maris* that Solomon operated his royal monopoly in horses and chariots. A rough memorandum in the Annals leaves the details of this trading adventure somewhat obscure:

Horses were imported from Egypt and Coa for Solomon; the royal merchants obtained them from Coa by purchase. Chariots were imported from Egypt for six hundred silver shekels each, and horses for a hundred and fifty; in the same way the merchants obtained them for export from all the kings of the Hittites and the kings of Aram.

If the first reference to 'Misraim' (Egypt) is, in fact, a mistaken reading for 'Musri', which most scholars now identify with the region at the north-eastern tip of the Mediterranean (later Cappadocia), Solomon seems to have acted as middleman for horses imported from the northern breeding grounds of Musri and Cilicia (Coa, or Kue) and for chariots imported from Egypt, for sale, perhaps, to the neighbouring Syrian states with Hamath as a trading centre.[11]

THE ROYAL CITIES

In view of the attractions of the *Via Maris* for armies as well as traders, it is not surprising that Solomon fortified its strategic

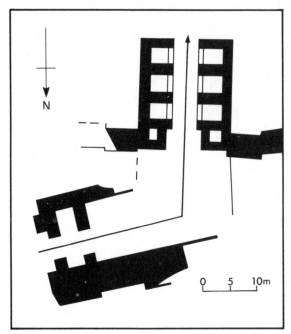

Fig. 9 Plan of the excavated Solomonic gate at Megiddo showing a six-chambered gate house virtually identical in design and dimensions with those of Hazor and Gezer. The 'outer gate' corresponds to that at Gezer. At Hazor, there are indications that the approach to the gate was angular or curved, but whether or not there was an 'outer gate' will not be known until this area has been excavated.

Fig. 10 Plan of the excavated Solomonic gate and casemate-wall at Hazor. The gate has six chambers, three on each side of the passage, with square towers in front. The casemates are 8–10·5 m long; the outer wall is 1·5–1·6 m thick and the inner wall 1·1 m thick. The space between the walls is 2·4–2·5 m. Each of the casemates has an entrance by the partition wall.

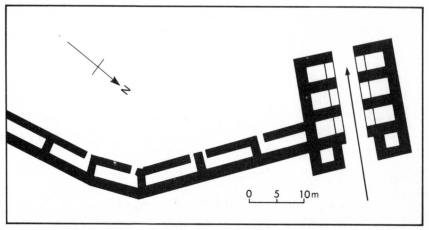

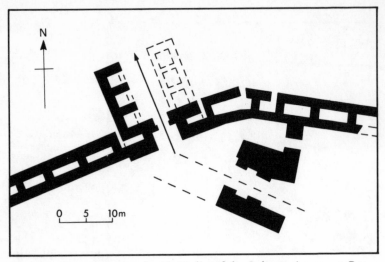

Fig. 11   Reconstruction by Y. Yadin of the Solomonic gate at Gezer. The plans of the casemate-wall and the gate are shown to be virtually identical with those of Megiddo and Hazor; details of construction, such as the dressing of the ashlar in the gate-jambs and the use of headers and stretchers, are also similar. Gezer had an 'outer-gate', which resembles that at Megiddo both in position and plan.

points: 'This is the record of the forced labour which King Solomon conscripted to build the house of the Lord, his own palace, the Millo, the wall of Jerusalem, and Hazor, Megiddo, and Gezer.'[12] Although it is improbable that Solomon's Jerusalem will ever be accessible to the archaeologist, excavations at Hazor, Megiddo and Gezer have recently revealed so distinctive a 'royal style' in this period that it can no longer be thought that the architecture of the capital is simply anybody's guess.

Megiddo, next to Jerusalem, must have been Solomon's principal pride and joy. Despite its decisive position as the guardian of the Carmel pass and the junction of the two northern branches of the *Via Maris*, Megiddo, like Hazor, had lain virtually deserted for over a century and a half when Solomon initiated his crash building programme. It is only in the last decade that the achievements of his reign have emerged clearly from the complex stratification of the site.

The thirteen-acre summit of the mound of Megiddo was

9 Part of the decoration of a platform on which Amenophis III sits enthroned in a painting from the tomb of an unknown official at Thebes (Dynasty XVIII). Syrians are grovelling at the feet of the Pharaoh. The most unusual feature is 'the open mouths showing the teeth, a trait which gives an expression of pain well suited to the abject position of the recumbent bodies'. (Davies and Gardiner, *Ancient Egyptian Paintings*).

10 Painting from the Theban tomb of a 'Scribe keeping account of the corn of Amun', that is, a temple official (Dynasty XVIII). The scribe on the left, with papyrus and palette, is registering the geese brought as tax; the farmers queue to prostrate themselves.

11   Ostracon from Tell Qasileh with Hebrew inscription (8th century BC). The inscription, 'Gold of Ophir for bēt hōron, thirty shekels', may refer either to Upper and Lower Beth-horon, used as a store city in the Solomonic period, or to the House (temple) of the Canaanite god Haurôn.

12   Painting from the tomb of Hapu (Dynasty XVIII). The chariot was built largely of wood—special kinds for each part —strips of leather, and various metals. The combination of rear axle, light body and wheels, and powerful draft animals brought about the perfect chariot.

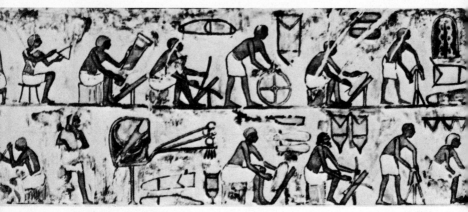

13   Plan of the 'New Palace' (excavation number 6000) and casemate-walls of Solomon's Megiddo. The rectangular building (28 × 21 m.) is constructed on the edge of the Tell and has an entrance on the south side. The plan, with its ceremonial hall and adjoining rooms, resembles the 'bît-hilani' style.

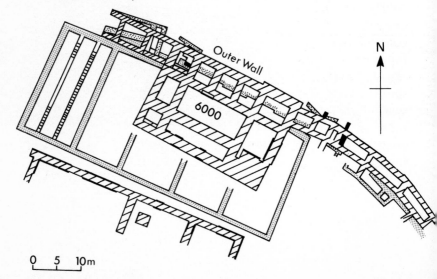

enclosed by a casemate wall, a type of fortification (consisting of two parallel walls linked by cross walls to form small rooms or 'casemates') which was repeated by Solomon's architects not only at Hazor and Gezer, but over the length and breadth of the kingdom – at Arad, Beth-shemesh, Eziongeber, and, it now appears, 'Ein Gev, a settlement of some size on the eastern shore of the Sea of Galilee.[13] Allowing for minor variations (explicable in terms of the vulnerability of the site), there is an extraordinary degree of uniformity in the dimensions of these casemate fortifications (outer wall five feet thick and inner wall four feet thick, with a seven-foot space between them), which suggests that Solomon's architects built to a standard pattern designed for speedy construction and relative cheapness. Many of them were replaced in the following century by thick solid walls, because, it is thought, they were found too weak to withstand the battering ram and the tunnelling of enemy sappers. The need for economy is also suggested by the curious fact that, both at Megiddo and Hazor, important public buildings were sited on the edge of the mound, so that their outer walls served as an integral part of the city-wall.

There was nothing cheap or weak, however, about the gates which Solomon's men built in his royal cities. The magnificent structure at Megiddo, with an outer gate between twin towers on the approach road, leading through a courtyard to the gate-house proper, an elaborate building designed with four sets of piers set into the casemate wall, all constructed in well-cut and beautifully bonded masonry, was for many years admired as a unique achievement. However, excavations at Hazor during the years 1955–58 and at Gezer since 1967 (the latter suggested by a superb piece of detective work on earlier archaeological data) have produced two more almost identical gate-houses erected by Solomon's architects. As with the related casemate walls, the measurements are so nearly the same for the gate in each of the three cities (Megiddo 68 feet long and 58 feet wide; Hazor 68 × 60; Gezer 65 × 54) that a single blueprint may safely be assumed.

In fact, the excavators of Hazor laid out the gate-plan of Megiddo on the surface of the site and, as if using a paper pattern, followed its lines in making their cuttings. When, in addition, the plan is seen to bear a close resemblance to Ezekiel's description of the east gate into the main court of the Jerusalem temple, it becomes fairly obvious that the royal architects were either markedly unimaginative, or cramped by a system which was highly centralized and rigidly controlled.[14]

As Solomon's civil servants were trained in the way of Egypt's bureaucracy, it is interesting but not altogether surprising to learn that the dimensions of these gates presuppose the Egyptian common cubit of 17·7 inches and not the slightly smaller Palestinian unit which was derived from it.[15] It would be unwise, however, to give too much weight to this kind of fingerprint, or to the suggestion that the great vertical shaft (116 feet deep) of Megiddo's water system was measured with a levelling instrument like the one found in the tomb of an Egyptian architect of the Ramesside period. In any case, although the ashlar gallery, representing the first stage of the city water works to give access to the spring, is now ascribed to Solomon's age, the shaft and tunnel are almost certainly a later feat of engineering.[16]

There can be no doubt, however, that recent excavations in the royal cities have fully confirmed the importance which the Annals give to them. Megiddo, it is evident, was rebuilt on a most ambitious scale with a whole series of official buildings, of which one on the north of the site is thought to have been a fort and another, on the south side, a palace. This 'southern palace', a complex (77 × 72 feet) constructed in fine ashlar masonry laid regularly in 'headers' and 'stretchers', may well have been the residence of the district governor. Further excavation at Megiddo in 1960 unearthed a second and slightly larger palace (the 'New Palace') built on the same plan, which, it has now been suggested, was designed for ceremonial use and borrowed from the so-called 'bît-hilani' style favoured by the architects of northern Syria.[17]

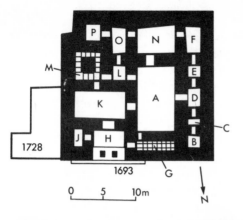

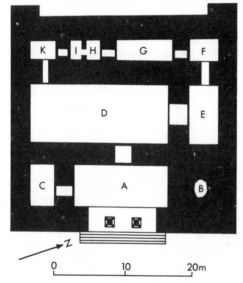

Fig. 12 Plan of the southern palace in Megiddo as reconstructed by D. Ussishkin. The building is surrounded on three sides by an open court, like the 'great court' in Jerusalem. Following the 'bît-hilani' plan, there is an entrance hall with portico (H) and adjoining room (J), which leads into the ceremonial hall (K). There was probably a staircase in the long narrow room to the right of the portico (G). An open court (A) is surrounded by living quarters, divided into two units on the west side (B, C, D, E, F) and on the south side (L, N, O, P). It is suggested that this Megiddo palace was a smaller version of Solomon's palace in Jerusalem.

Fig. 13 Ground-plan of Hilani III in Zinjirli (Samal, the Aramean city of North Syria), as reconstructed by D. Ussishkin. Following the 'bît-hilani' plan, there is an entrance hall with portico (A) and adjoining room (C), which leads into the ceremonial hall (D). There was probably a staircase in the tower on the right of the portico (B).

The 'bît-hilani' has been described as 'a palace with two long narrow rooms, both with their main axis parallel to the façade. The first is a portico with from one to three columns, often placed at the top of a low flight of steps. Stairs to the upper storey are set to one side of the portico.'[18] The second and larger of the two rooms of the southern palace (26×13 feet) had access to an open court, surrounded by small symmetrical chambers probably designed as living quarters.

73

THE JERUSALEM PALACE

For all their ambiguities, the provincial palaces of Megiddo are the best clue we possess to the character of Solomon's palace in Jerusalem and, in view of the degree of standardization adopted by his architects, similarity between the two is intrinsically probable. On the reasonable assumption that the 'House of the Forest of Lebanon' was an independent building, the biblical description of Solomon's palace begins with 'the colonnade', an oblong structure (83 × 50 feet) with pillars.[19] A 'bît-hilani' plan would then suggest that the 'Hall of Judgment' was a large room beyond and parallel to 'the colonnade' and its considerable size is confirmed by the fact that it housed the 'great throne of ivory' with six steps.[20] The royal living quarters – 'his own house where he was to reside' and 'the house he made for Pharaoh's daughter' – were built 'in a court set back from the colonnade', as they were at Megiddo. The Annals are at pains to emphasize the superior quality of the masonry of these buildings – 'all these were made of heavy blocks of stone, hewn to measure and trimmed with the saw on the inner and outer sides . . . at the base were heavy stones, massive blocks, some ten and some eight cubits [17 and 13 feet] in size' – and so, as has been pointed out, were the excavators of the smaller provincial palace at Megiddo:

The foundations were composed chiefly of irregularly shaped but exceptionally large stones (averaging about half a meter in diameter), but many of the facing stones were hewn square. . . . The elevation of wall 1649 [the west wall of the palace] shows quite conclusively that the outer face of at least the lower part of the superstructure was constructed of solid ashlar masonry.[21]

THE HYPOSTYLE HALL

The adjacent 'House of the Forest of Lebanon', on the contrary, conforms to no standard design which has so far been identified. Analogies have ranged far and wide – from Amarna in the fourteenth century B C to Athens in the fourth century B C, with a new favourite candidate in the audience

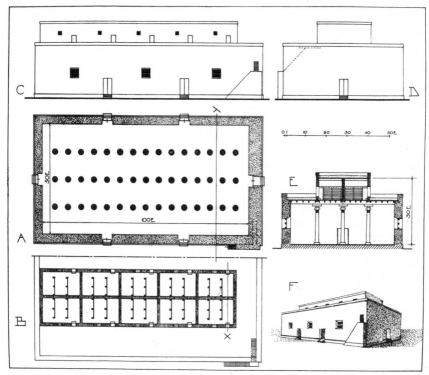

Fig. 14 Reconstruction of the 'House of the Forest of Lebanon' (I Kgs. 7.2–5) by Th. A. Busink. The scale is given in cubits; a cubit is approximately 50 cm.

chamber of the Great Fortress of Boğazköy, the capital of the ancient Hittite empire. Such speculations arise from the fact that the biblical data are too scrappy and ambiguous to serve as the basis for any confident reconstruction of the building. Essentially, it was a light and lofty hypostyle hall, with four times the floor-space of the Temple, designed, as its name suggests, round three (or four) rows of cedar columns. Whether or not it is judged to have had an upper storey depends entirely on the interpretation of Hebrew terms of uncertain meaning; the most recent translation of the text (in the New English Bible) disallows an upper storey, whereas the most recent reconstruction of the building courageously indicates its shape and size.[22] Solomon, we are told, kept his shields and bucklers there, and at the end of the eighth century BC the prophet Isaiah spoke of 'the weapons stored in the House of the Forest'. If the building was, indeed, intended as a treasury and magazine, small storerooms upstairs gain in plausibility.[23]

PHOENICIAN CRAFTSMEN

Nothing is known to have survived from any of Solomon's buildings in Jerusalem, with the possible and fascinating exception of 'a tumble of ashlar blocks . . . and amongst them two halves of a pilaster capital of Proto-Ionic type'. This recent find adds interest to the fact that a number of similar Proto-Ionic capitals were excavated at Megiddo, some of which, at least, are held to come from the Solomonic city.[24] Although further examples discovered at Samaria and Hazor may be definitely ascribed to the royal architects of Omri and Ahab (876–850 BC), this does not determine either the provenance of the style or the period of its use, since during the last decade no less than seven more specimens have been excavated at Beth-Haccherem (Ramat Raḥel) in Judah, where they decorated a palace built on virgin soil at the end of the seventh century BC. The picture is further complicated by the discovery of similar capitals in Cyprus of the seventh or sixth century BC in a form elaborated by curled palmettes, lotus plants and sphinxes.[25] This range of places and dates makes it probable that it was Solomon who introduced the Proto-Ionic capital in his buildings at Jerusalem and Megiddo and that both in his time and later the royal architects were Phoenician.

The sudden efflorescence in the tenth century BC of a finished (if stereotyped) architectural style executed by skilled craftsmen, following, as it did, a period of sharp decline from Canaanite standards, which has been observed on so many Palestinian sites, points unmistakably both to the initial material and cultural poverty of the monarchy and to Solomon's obsessive determination to change the situation overnight. Such instant transformations are accomplished only by calling in experts, and it was natural that Solomon should have looked to Hiram of Tyre to supply him with technical 'wisdom'.[26]

The Phoenicians were already to the Levant what the Japanese have recently become to the western world – a people of enormous energy and enterprise, whose skill in combining precise techniques with mass production was equalled only by their ingenuity in finding markets and pleasing their customers. Their commercial instinct, no less than their mixed ancestry and wide seafaring contacts, made them *par excellence* the adaptors of other people's traditions, so that to describe Solomon's buildings as 'Phoenician' is to praise the quality of their workmanship rather than to identify with any precision the style of their architecture. Although in the minor arts, as illustrated by their ivory carving, it could be argued that the Phoenicians' capacity for adaptation and cultural synthesis was in itself creative, they were never the disseminators of a single coherent style, whether in art or in life and, in consequence, their influence on the nations to whom they sold their goods and their services was little more than marginal. Tyre's contribution to Solomon's new nation was of a totally different order from that of Egypt. Even in its decline, the ancient tradition of Egypt was strong enough to inspire genuine if ill-conceived imitation; the men of Tyre were simply hired to put up buildings in the current international style.

THE TEMPLE

If, as has been said of the Phoenician ivories, the temple of Solomon was also 'the product of commercial minds', alive to the need for trimming according to the customer's requirements, it is not surprising that its architectural tradition and the religious significance of its detail should have proved so difficult to determine. Since the first temple ever to be excavated in Phoenicia was discovered as recently as 1972 and according to preliminary reports was quite a small building

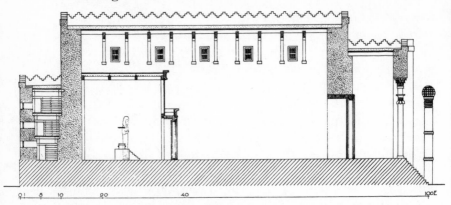

Fig. 15   Reconstruction of a longitudinal section of Solomon's Temple by Th. A. Busink. The scale is given in cubits; one cubit is about 50 cm.

Fig. 16   Reconstruction of the ground-plan of Solomon's Temple by Th. A. Busink. The scale is given in cubits; one cubit is approximately 50 cm.

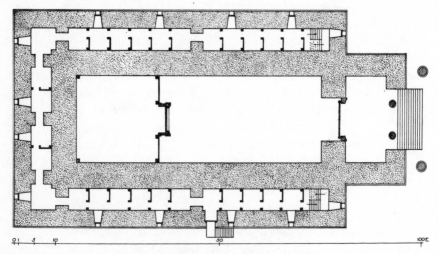

(24 feet long and 12 feet wide),[27] it is to be expected that Solomon's temple will continue to need more than one prototype to account for its hybrid character. It does, however, fall decisively into one of the two main categories evolved for studying the architecture of the Ancient Near

East. 'The house . . . was sixty cubits [100 feet] long by twenty cubits [33 feet] broad, and its height was thirty cubits [50 feet].' It was, that is to say, a *Langraum* – an oblong room with the entrance in one of the short sides and its axis along the line of approach – as distinct from a *Breitraum* – an oblong room with the entrance in the middle of one of the long sides and its axis across the line of approach.[28] In this respect, the temple of the ninth century BC excavated in 1936 at Tell Tainat in northern Syria provides the nearest analogy so far discovered.[29] Like the Jerusalem temple, the 'long room' at Tell Tainat had an 'inner sanctuary' at its west end with a 'vestibule' at its east end and was a relatively small building in an elaborate palace complex.

It has been claimed that the Hazor temples of the fourteenth and thirteenth centuries BC, with their vestibule, sanctuary and inner sanctuary, are significant prototypes of Solomon's temple, but their development and final plan clearly show that they fall into the *Breitraum* category and differ basically in that the inner sanctuary forms the principal room and is designed to accommodate worshippers.[30] The astonishing discovery in 1962 of a temple of the Solomonic period at Arad in the far south – the first Israelite sanctuary to be

Fig. 17
Isometric plan of the temple and palace at Tell Tainat, ancient Hattina in North Syria, between Aleppo and Antioch (9th–8th century BC). The temple (in the background) is a *Langraum* (24 × 13 m). The palace illustrates the 'bît-hilani' plan.

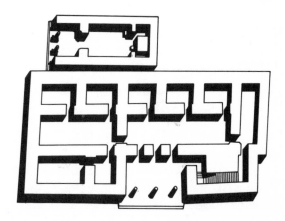

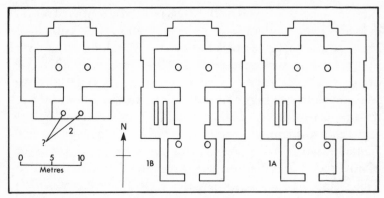

Fig. 18   Plan of three temples excavated at Hazor, as reconstructed by
Th. A. Busink. On the left (2), the oldest temple plan, used from the
17th to the 15th century BC, is of the *Breitraum* type. The broad hall
(13·5 × 8·9 m) had a roof supported by two capitals, with a small niche
on the north side and a wide entrance porch on the south side. In the
centre, (1B), the new plan of the 14th century BC temple shows a
development of the entrance on the south side. The porch itself is a wide
room (9·8 × 4·8 m) with, perhaps, two pillars near the inner entrance.
On the right (1A), the plan of the 13th century BC temple is virtually
identical with that of its predecessor, except for the expansion of the
middle room eastwards. Two pillars were found *in situ* inside the porch,
which (like 'Jachin and Boaz' in Solomon's temple) appear to have had
no structural function.

excavated – further reduces the hope of relating the
Jerusalem temple to a native Canaanite–Palestinian tradition.
The main sanctuary of Arad was a small 'broad room'
(9 × 30 feet) and the inner sanctuary a mere niche at the top
of three steps.[31]

The inner sanctuary

The inner sanctuary at the west end of Solomon's Temple is
problematical but quite different: 'In the innermost part of
the house he partitioned off a space of twenty cubits with
cedar boards from floor to rafters and made of it an inner
shrine, to be the Most Holy Place.' If, as this description
suggests and as the latest reconstruction emphasizes,[32] the

inner sanctuary – a perfect cube with sides of 33 feet – was not an integral part of the structure of the building, it is possible that it represents an Israelite innovation modelled on the tent-sanctuary which previously housed the Ark. Any such concession to ancient religious tradition was, however, fundamentally qualified (if not vitiated) by the two alien cherubim, free-standing figures made of olive-wood nearly 17 feet in wing span and height, which guarded the Ark and completely dominated the inner sanctuary. These winged creatures, upon which Israel was taught to believe that God was invisibly enthroned, are a variety of the Ancient Near Eastern sphinx, often represented in the Phoenician ivories as guarding the Sacred Tree or, as in an inlay from Arslan Tash, the figure of a god.[33]

Fig. 19 Reconstruction of the exterior of Solomon's Temple by Th. A. Busink.

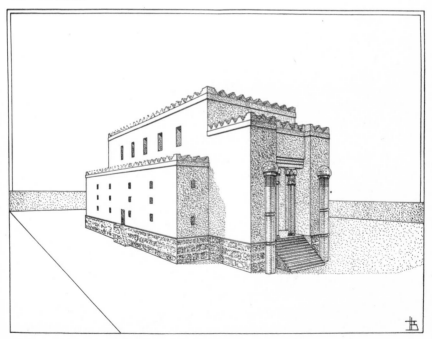

The sanctuary

Although Hiram's craftsmen are not explicitly said to have been responsible for the interior decoration of the sanctuary, the Egyptianizing motifs described in the biblical record – carved figures of cherubim, palm-trees, and open flowers – are so well illustrated by Phoenician ivories that there can be little doubt about the workmanship.[34] From the fourteenth to at least the eighth century BC, the craft of ivory carving flourished in Syria and the Phoenician cities and the work of the latter is distinctive for its wholesale adaptation of Egyptian themes. The designs of the Phoenician craftsmen are well known to us from a large group of ivories, carved between 1350 and 1150 BC, discovered at Megiddo, collections found at Samaria and Arslan Tash in Syria, generally ascribed to the ninth century BC, and the marvellously rich Assyrian caches excavated at Nimṛud, which are thought largely to have been carved between 850 and 700 BC.[35]

The extreme conservatism of the ivory carvers in their choice of subjects means that, allowing for minor developments in their treatment, work of different periods conveys with sufficient accuracy an impression of the decoration which Solomon commissioned for the interior of his buildings. The palm-tree, for example, appears in a comparable stylized form in ivory plaques from Samaria and Nimrud and is a recurrent feature of both ivory and metalwork in the 'Phoenician' style. Floral decorations abound. An open-work carving from Nimrud, probably designed as a panel for a chair, nicely represents interlaced branches of flowering rosettes, palmettes and papyrus, but the most beautiful example of the use of flowers in the Assyrian collection is the famous pair of ivories depicting the 'Ethiopian and the Lioness'. The figures here are set against a background of alternating Egyptian lilies and papyrus flowers, the blue lilies being made of *lapis lazuli* incrustation and the red papyrus flowers of polished dome-shaped cornelians.

Another masterpiece from Nimrud illustrates the 'figures of cherubim', which were carved on the cedar walls of

Solomon's sanctuary. Designed to decorate an elaborate chair or throne, this plaque depicts a sphinx in Pharaonic head-cloth and crown, wearing a Phoenician-style apron. The lunette framework still bears traces of the gold overlay which the carvers of the Assyrian ivories applied so lavishly and which, the excavator suggests, not only 'made a meretricious appeal to a *nouveau riche* court', but represents a practice inherited from 'an older, and perhaps commoner, woodwork technique which the carver had devised in order to conceal knots and defects in the graining'.[36] Both parts of this explanation illuminate the interior decoration of Solomon's temple, which the record represents as an unrelieved glitter of gold: 'He carved cherubim, palms, and open flowers, overlaying them evenly with gold over the carving . . . the whole house he overlaid with gold until it was all covered' – including the floor, for which there was good Egyptian precedent. The inscriptions of the Pharaohs frequently enlarge on the lavish use of rich materials and claim that 'silver, electrum and gold sheets line wooden doors, stone floors, parts of low reliefs, and pyramidions'.[37]

The vestibule
The vestibule of the temple, projecting some 17 feet at the east end of the main building, seems to have been supported on pillars ('The capitals at the tops of the pillars in the vestibule were shaped like lilies and were four cubits [7 feet] high') to form an open portico. This feature is reminiscent of the 'bît-hilani' colonnade of Solomon's palaces at both Megiddo and Jerusalem, and, as the Tell Tainat sanctuary confirms, the architects of northern Syria also used it in designing their temples. It is reasonable to speculate that the lily-shaped capitals of these pillars were in the ubiquitous Proto-Ionic style, of which, as the Phoenician ivories amply illustrate, the distinctive double volute is derived from 'the turned-down sepals of the Egyptian "southflower", the so-called Lily of Upper Egypt'.[38] An interesting Egyptian example of a capital in this style was discovered in the mortuary temple of

Ramesses III at Medinet Habu. Here the brilliantly coloured pillar is surmounted by three superimposed capitals: at the bottom a half-open lotus capital, from which springs a smaller capital of open papyrus, and at the top a still smaller double-voluted lily capital. This type of three-staged capital was imitated from the wooden ones often represented in the wall-paintings of Theban tombs.[39]

The pillars

In front of the vestibule, two free-standing 30-foot bronze pillars, bearing the names *Jachin* (or *Jackun*, meaning 'It shall stand') and *Boaz* (or *Booz*, meaning 'In strength') dominated the approach to the Temple. Herodotus reported that the temple of Heracles at Tyre had 'two pillars, one of refined gold, one of emerald', a feature which, centuries earlier, the Phoenicians had probably borrowed from Egypt, where it was customary to celebrate a festival by erecting two obelisks in front of the temple of Amon-Re. A building inscription of Amenophis III illustrates not only this practice, but also the vulgar record-breaking spirit and flashy lavishness which Solomon made such efforts to emulate:

I made other monuments for Amon, of which the like has never occurred. I built for thee . . . an august place of fine gold, a resting place for my father in all his feasts. It is embellished with fine sandstone and worked with gold throughout. Its pavement is decorated with silver, and all its doorways with gold. Two great obelisks have been erected, one on each side, so that my father [i.e. the sun-god] may appear between them, while I am in his retinue. I have sacrificed to him thousands of oxen. . . .[40]

The capitals of *Jachin* and *Boaz*, which added eight feet to their total height, are elaborately described in the Annals as bowl-shaped and decorated with ornamental network, lily-work and rows of pomegranates. It is improbable that ingenious reconstructions of these artistic monstrosities will improve on a lamp shaped like a capital found as long ago as 1908 at Megiddo, if it is appropriately enriched with pomegranates, like the charming ivory set which were recently found in a well at Nimrud.[41]

METALWORK

The 'great skill and ingenuity' of the half-Israelite bronze-worker, whom Solomon hired from Tyre, has so far defeated scholars attempting to fathom the gigantic cast metal tank known as 'The Sea', which stood in the Temple forecourt.[42] On the assumption that the scribe made the mistake of using the formula for calculating the capacity of a sphere instead of a hemisphere, it is possible to reduce the quantity of water it allegedly held from 10,000 to 5,000 gallons, but even this more modest figure, coupled with the fact that it stood some fifteen feet off the ground, removes the object from any practical use to the realm of symbolism. It is at least clear that 'The Sea' was never designed in the first place for a region where water was a precious commodity; but if 'the use of designs without concern for their original meaning is', as a leading expert holds, 'characteristic of Phoenician metalwork', it would be hazardous to suppose that Solomon was attracted by some cosmic significance given to this piece in its native context, any more than that he interpreted as fertility symbols the twelve bulls on which it stood.[43]

Solomon's expert also cast ten highly ornate bronze trolleys, which the Annals describe with the loving detail one normally associates with the owners of vintage cars.[44] With their 200-gallon basins full of water, notwithstanding the fact that the wheels were constructed like those of one of Solomon's splendid new chariots – 'their axles, hubs, spokes, and felloes being all of cast metal' – it seems probable that they were not designed for mobility and were simply lined up as static status symbols on each side of the court of the temple.

This lavish display of costly bronze work poses difficult problems about both the origin of the raw material and the technique of its processing. Although grandiose claims about 'King Solomon's Mines' at Ezion-geber have now been abandoned, the mineral wealth of the Wadi Arabah region, lying to the north of the Israelite port, is still thought to have made a major contribution to the royal treasury. Cupriferous sandstone, nodules of silica-bound copper-ores, and pottery crucibles coated with slag found over the years in this area give clear evidence of mining and smelting. Although it is impossible to estimate the scale of these operations, it is unlikely, as once was thought, that they supplied copper in quantities sufficient, not only for the temple-builders' bronze-working in the Jordan valley, but even for export in those 'ships of Tarshish' which regularly set sail from Ezion-geber.[45]

The name of these merchantmen is an old crux, but it may, nevertheless, provide a clue to the problems raised by Solomon's extravagant enterprise. 'Tarshish' is the name not of some distant port on the Red Sea route, but of a mining region in the Mediterranean. It had come to be used by the Phoenicians to describe the type of freighter they employed in their Mediterranean trading, and it was this same type of ship which the men of Tyre built for Solomon's Red Sea traffic. A savage oracle on Babylon's defeat of Tyre in 574 B C, now embodied in the book of Isaiah, helps fill in the background:

> The ships of Tarshish howl, for the harbour is sacked;
> the port of entry from Kittim [Cyprus] is swept away. . . .
> When the news is confirmed in Egypt
> her people sway in anguish at the fate of Tyre.
> Make your way to Tarshish, they say,
> howl, you who dwell by the sea-coast.
> Is this your busy city, ancient in story,
> on whose voyages you were carried to settle far away? . . .
> Though you arise and cross over to Kittim,
> even there you shall find no rest.[46]

The anonymous prophet comes near, it seems, to identifying Tarshish with Cyprus, but that may be because Cyprus was the first and last port of call for merchantmen voyaging

14　Proto-Ionic capital from Ramat Rahel, the site of a royal fortress near Jerusalem built (probably) in the 7th century BC.

15　Limestone stela in the form of a Proto-Ionic capital from Golgoi, Cyprus (late 6th century BC).

16　Ivory handle of a fan or fly-whisk (10 × 3·3 cm.) from Nimrud (8th century BC). It is decorated with three superimposed volutes and at the top has three tubes for holding bristles. The panel shows two kneeling figures touching the sacred palmette.

17　Ivory inlay (height 8 cm.) from Arslan Tash, depicting a god on a stylized flower guarded by two sphinxes (8th century BC). The free rendering of Egyptian themes in the ivories makes it difficult to judge whether the god is 'the young sun-god appearing in a lotus from primeval waters, or the birth of Horus in the marshes, where Isis had hidden him from his enemies'. (Frankfort, *The Art and Architecture of the Ancient Orient*).

18　Open-work ivory plaque (11·8 × 5·2 cm.) from Nimrud (8th century BC). It is shaped as a stylized palm tree, like plaques from Samaria.

19　One of a pair of ivory plaques (length 10·5 cm.) from Nimrud (8th century BC). The lioness is modelled on Egyptian representations and on the top there is a letter in Phoenician script. 'Gold leaf has been applied lavishly to the outlines and stems of the flowers, and the negro's dress and hair which is formed by inserted ivory pegs. The lotus flowers are inlaid with lapis bedded in a mortar of calcium carbonate and blue powdered frit. The papyrus flowers are inlaid with carnelian.' (Barnett, *The Nimrud Ivories*).

further west. Traditionally, Tarshish has been identified with Tartessos in southern Spain, but there is no agreed archaeological evidence of Phoenician influence in this region earlier than the eighth century B C. It has been concluded, therefore, that Tarshish, which is represented in the Assyrian inscriptions as being at the opposite end of the Mediterranean to Cyprus, referred to western Mediterranean mining areas in general.[47] On the main issue, however, there is no doubt: if, as seems probable, the local supply of copper from the Wadi Arabah was limited, Solomon's Phoenician bronze-worker could readily have augmented it from his countrymen's traditional Tarshish trade.

The importance of Cyprus itself as a source of the metal in the Late Bronze Age was vividly illustrated in 1960, when skin-diving archaeologists discovered a ton of copper ingots and about half a hundredweight of tin in a small Cypriot cargo boat which sank off the south coast of Turkey about 1200 B C. The ingots were shaped like ox-hides with a large carrying handle at each corner. These handles distinguish them from an earlier design represented in fifteenth-century Egyptian tomb paintings and identify them as the type brought to Cyprus at the end of the thirteenth century B C by the Mycenaeans, who had probably borrowed the convention from Crete.[48] Although it is thought that the wrecked Cypriot ship was on her way to Greece, it is not inconceivable that similar cargo boats brought copper direct to Israel in Solomon's time, since the excavation of Tell Qasileh on the northern bank of the Yarkon River has established that it was the site of an active port in the tenth century B C, with a tradition of copper refining and, on the evidence of imported wares, close commercial relations with Cyprus and the Phoenician cities. When, therefore, Hiram of Tyre made arrangements with Solomon for the delivery of his timber – 'My men shall bring down the logs from Lebanon to the sea and I will make them up into rafts to be floated to the place you appoint' – it is probable that Tell Qasileh was the chosen port.[49]

The traffic between Cyprus and the mainland carried, however, not only copper ingots but craftsmen and their traditional skills. A number of bronze cauldron stands with openwork panels, dating from the twelfth to eleventh century B C, have been excavated at Cypriot sites and it is immediately obvious that they are the kind of trolley which was made for Solomon's temple: 'They had panels set in frames; on these panels were portrayed lions, oxen, and cherubim . . . above and below . . . were fillets of hammered work of spiral design.'[50] These inter-connections were further demonstrated in 1964 by the discovery at Tell es-Sa'idiyeh of a rich tomb deposit which included a bronze tripod comparable to examples from Cyprus and a bronze cauldron (not so far found on the island), which is dated in the thirteenth to the twelfth century B C. The grave also yielded a bronze wine set (bowl, strainer and juglet) such as was found at Amarna and (to hazard a guess) impressed the Queen of Sheba when she visited Solomon.[51] The fact that Tell es-Sa'idiyeh is now generally identified with Zarethan makes the connection with the temple metalwork uncannily close, since it is recorded that 'the pots, the shovels, and the tossing bowls – all these objects . . . were of bronze, burnished work. In the Plain of the Jordan the king cast them, *in the foundry between Succoth and Zarethan.*'[52] It is not unreasonable to suppose that Zarethan had once been a prosperous bronze-working centre and that Solomon's Phoenician craftsmen gave it new life when they settled down there to turn out the old designs. Their arrival may even account for the fact that the residential area so far excavated (dated in the eighth century B C) reveals a straight street of almost identical houses – a phenomenon sufficiently remarkable to encourage speculation about the town-planning department of Solomon's centralized administration.

THE IVORY THRONE

The extravagant assertion of Solomon's scribes that the metalwork of the temple broke all previous records ('so great was the quantity of bronze . . . that the weight of it was beyond all reckoning') is matched by their claim about the unprecedented grandeur of his 'great throne of ivory overlaid with fine gold', which stood in the Hall of Judgment: 'Nothing like it had ever been made for any monarch.'[53] In fact, no exact parallel has been found for this grandiose piece of furniture, set on a dais and approached by six steps, each with a lion at either end, with yet more lions standing by the arms of the throne, and the head of a calf at the back. There is good evidence that the Phoenicians made elaborate thrones with sphinxes for arms, so that the king, as the psalmist says of God, was, indeed, 'throned on the cherubim'.[54] A stone sarcophagus carved for a thirteenth-century king of Byblos depicts him seated in just such a sphinx-throne, another example of which may be seen in the well-known fourteenth-century ivory inlay from Megiddo. Although it is probable that these Phoenician examples give a fair impression of the majesty to which Solomon aspired, there is nothing to indicate that the lion standing by each of the arms of his throne was, in fact, a *winged* lion. The best illustration of the biblical data is to be found in the portable chairs in which the Pharaohs were carried in state. Akhenaten (1379–1362 BC) is flanked by splendidly realistic lions in tomb paintings from Amarna and, two centuries later, Ramesses III is depicted in a chair guarded by both lions and sphinxes. The evidence for this decoration goes back at least to the reign of Tuthmosis III, and it appears to have been so well-established a style as to cast doubt on the view that the thrones in the Pharaohs' palaces were comparatively simple.[55]

The 'head of a calf' at the back of Solomon's throne was too reminiscent of the idolatrous golden calves of Jeroboam for the orthodoxy of later copyists, and so the offending text was variously changed to 'the top of the throne was *rounded behind*', to the less objectionable 'lamb' and, finally, to the harmless 'footstool'.[56] It is possible that these suspicions were not without remote justification, since the representation of a cow suckling its calf, a substitute and symbol for many varieties of mother goddess, permeated the whole of the Ancient Near East and is often found in the Phoenician ivories of Arslan Tash and Nimrud.[57] The finest example of many dozens of Nimrud plaques depicting this subject still shows traces of gold on the papyrus flowers and lotus buds, which, in this context, recalls the fact that the ivory panels of Solomon's throne were 'overlaid with fine gold'. Whatever the original significance of the calf's head, 'it would seem that a preoccupation with richness of decoration rather than with religion' explains this no less than the other works of the king's busy commercial artists.[58]

THE COURT

The throne was the central symbol of a court of fabulous opulence. In a society which accepted polygamy, the possession of a large harim was an obvious way of displaying

Fig. 20 Painting from the Theban tomb of Nefer-hotep (Dynasty XVIII). Meryet-Re, the wife of the honoured official, has been received by the queen in King Ay's harim, where she accepts gifts from an upper window. The scene presents the house in a combined front and side elevation and shows nurses looking after the children, with an abundant supply of food and drink, which the maids in the garden (top left) have already started to enjoy.

wealth, as a later deuteronomic critic of the monarchy implies in his two-fold warning: 'He shall not acquire many wives and so be led astray; nor shall he acquire great quantities of silver and gold for himself.' It is a writer of the same school who credits Solomon with seven hundred wives and three hundred concubines – a suspiciously round number, exploiting for a stricture what was probably originally given out as a boast.[59] Once again, it is the reign of Amenophis III which provides convincing parallels. According to the Amarna letters, he ordered from the king of Gezer forty 'beautiful women' at forty silver shekels each and, in addition, as he lost no time in announcing to the kingdom at large, three hundred and seventeen women accompanied from Mitanni the princess who came to join his harim. Queen Tiy, however, was his 'great royal spouse' and, like the Pharaoh's daughter at Solomon's court, enjoyed the privilege of a private palace.[60]

Music

The new cosmopolitan atmosphere of the Jerusalem court is revealed quite incidentally in a note about Solomon's imports of almug wood, which he used 'to make stools for the house of the Lord and for the royal palace, *as well as harps and lutes for the singers*'. The probability that this is a reference to court entertainment rather than liturgical music in the temple is suggested by the claim that Solomon's songs 'numbered a thousand and five' and further supported by the reply of old Barzillai in the Succession Story, when David invites him to spend his remaining years as a member of his household: 'Your servant is far too old to go up with your majesty to Jerusalem. I am already eighty; and I cannot tell good from bad. I cannot taste what I eat or drink; I cannot hear the voices of men and women singing.'[61]

Professional musicians were a *sine qua non* of palace life in the Ancient Near East and are found pleasingly illustrated in the decoration of a number of ivory ointment boxes discovered at Nimrud. These beautiful little objects depict a group of men and women playing lyre, drum and flute before the court (as some of the boxes explicitly indicate), and details of their style, together with the crisp technique of the carving, are thought to date them in the eighth century BC.[62] The heavy Egyptian wigs of the men show that such scenes ultimately derived from the court of the Pharaohs, from which, according to an ancient Jewish legend, Solomon's wife brought a thousand musical instruments as part of her dowry. Notwithstanding the fact that the portable lyre (which is preferable as a translation to the heavy 'harp' of the New English Bible) was introduced to Egypt from Asia and is first represented in the hands of an Asiatic in the famous Beni Hasan tomb painting of about 1890 BC, the instrument was thoroughly naturalized during the New Kingdom and everything suggests that it was from his father-in-law that Solomon acquired professional musicians to keep the courtiers entertained in his new Jerusalem.[63]

Clever talk

Another favourite form of court entertainment was learned and witty conversation, characterized by that perverse delight in riddles and comparable displays of verbal dexterity which is now conveniently sublimated by the crossword puzzle. Such after-dinner sessions are reflected in more serious vein in the *Letter of Aristeas*, a fascinating piece of apologetic written towards the end of the second century BC by an educated Jew of Alexandria familiar with the Egyptian court. Here, the conversation at table between the king and his guests on all kinds of moral and religious questions amounts in the end to a pattern for rulers reminiscent of the Egyptian scribal instructions.[64] An even better example from the second century BC is the contest of wits at the Persian court of Darius now embodied in what the English Apocrypha calls the First Book of Esdras. It recounts how after dinner three young courtiers address themselves to the problem of judging which of all things is the strongest: 'One wrote "Wine is the strongest", the second wrote "The king is strongest", and the third wrote "Women are strongest, but truth conquers all".' The statements in which the three competitors defend their choice before the king are models of courtly speech.[65]

The great antiquity of this kind of court entertainment may be illustrated by an Egyptian work of royalist propaganda now known as the *Prophecy of Neferty*. This flattering account of how the order and prosperity of the kingdom were re-established after a period of anarchy was, in fact, written to support Ammenemes I (1991–1962 BC), the first king of the new Twelfth Dynasty, but it was given the authority which attached to prophecy in the ancient world by the device (adopted later by the author of the book of Daniel) of representing it as having been delivered some six hundred years earlier by a wise scribe introduced to the court in order to entertain the king. The setting of the work is the request made by King Sneferu (c. 2613 BC) that his courtiers should 'seek out for me a son of yours who is wise, or a brother of yours who is competent, or a friend of yours who has performed a good deed, one who may say to me *a few fine words or choice speeches, at the hearing of which my majesty may be entertained*'. And so Neferty, a lector-priest and man of rank, described as 'that wise man of the east', is brought before the king.[66]

At the court of Solomon, such entertainment, it is said, was provided by the king himself:

Solomon's wisdom surpassed that of all the men of the east and of all Egypt. For he was wiser than any man, wiser than Ethan the Ezrahite, and Heman, Kalcol, and Darda, the sons of Mahol; his fame spread among all the surrounding nations. He uttered three thousand proverbs, and his songs numbered a thousand and five. He discoursed of trees, from the cedar of Lebanon down to the marjoram that grows out of the wall, of beasts and birds, of reptiles and fishes.[67]

There is no means of deciding and there is no need to decide which items in this scribal testimonial should be ascribed to the clever conversation of the court and which to the more businesslike syllabuses of the schools. Solomon's courtiers were, as in Egypt, also his schoolmasters and it is for their derivative tradition of scribal culture that international fame is being claimed. Even the book of Proverbs, of which the earnest didacticism is more easily associated with classes before lunch than conversation after dinner, includes a number of riddles derived from the international courtly tradition. Just as the young men of the court of Darius proposed three (or, rather, four) answers to their teasing question, so the unidentified wit of Proverbs offers his *bon mot* about sex:

> Three things there are which are too wonderful for me,
> > four which I do not understand:
> > the way of a vulture in the sky,
> > the way of a serpent on the rock,
> > the way of a ship out at sea,
> > and the way of a man with a girl.[68]

Of the topics covered by Solomon and the Queen of Sheba we are not informed. However, the lavish context of the encounter, when he 'answered all her questions; not one of them was too abstruse for the king to answer', suggests that, as well as discussing the economics of the Red Sea traffic, the royal pair engaged in elegant courtly badinage, of which, no doubt, the Islamic and Ethiopian legends made too much.

20 Ivory panel (19 × 15 cm.), designed to decorate an elaborate chair or throne, from Nimrud (8th century BC). The winged sphinx with the body of a lion and the head of a man is set in a lunette framework overlaid with gold. The style shows a mixture of three artistic traditions: Egyptian in the Pharaonic head-cloth and crown, Phoenician in the apron, and Syrian in the broad features of the face. The voluted palmettes above and below the body may be compared to the ubiquitous Proto-Ionic capital (cf. Plate 14).

21 Fragment of a limestone engaged cluster-column (height 110 cm.) from the temple of Ramesses III at Medinet Habu. Three capitals are superimposed—'lily' over papyrus over lotus. The lilies are painted bright blue and red; the papyrus are blue-green with yellow sepals; the lotus blossoms are blue with sepals in blue and green.

22 Object in soft, grey limestone now generally identified as a lamp (height 23 cm., diameter of the top 16·2 cm.) from Megiddo (stratum VI).

23 One of the forty copper ingots of the so-called 'ox-hide' shape excavated from a Cypriot ship, which was wrecked about 1200 BC in Cape Gelidonya in south-west Turkey. The 'ox-hide' ingots in the cargo averaged 60 × 45 cm. and 20·6 kg.

24 Bronze wheeled cauldron-stand from Larnaka, Cyprus. The open-work sides show the pillar of a temple guarded by sphinxes.

26 Relief from the temple of Ramesses III at Medinet Habu (Dynasty XX). Mounted on a portable throne, the king is setting forth from his palace to participate in the ceremonies of the Feast of Min. The throne is flanked by a lion and a sphinx and, behind it, two goddesses extend their wings to serve as arm-rests.

27 One of many open-work ivory plaques (8·7 × 7·7 cm.) from Nimrud depicting a cow suckling its calf (8th century BC). Traces of gold remain on the papyrus flowers and lotus buds.

5 Stone sarcophagus of hiram from Byblos (13th ntury BC). The king sits on sphinx-throne before a rocession of men bringing im food and drink. The ene may reflect the gyptian funerary feast; the order of lotus buds and owers is clearly derived om Egypt.

28 The central plaque (24 × 12 cm.) of an ivory panel, composed of
six double-sided plaques, from a bed in the palace of Ras Shamra
(cf. Plate 44). It was discovered alongside a scarab announcing the
marriage of Amenophis III and may be dated *c.* 1400 BC. The plaque
depicts a winged and horned goddess suckling two identical male
figures. The latter have been interpreted either as a double representation of the young king of Ugarit, who is depicted on other plaques of
the panel, or as divine figures.

CHAPTER FIVE

Education in wisdom

THE FIRST unambiguous reference to an Israelite school occurs no earlier than the beginning of the second century B C in the book Ecclesiasticus: 'Come to me, you who need instruction, and lodge in my house of learning.'[1] 'The Wisdom of Jesus ben Sira' (to give the work its original title) is a fascinating educational manual compiled by the genial master of this Jerusalem school from the legacy of a long didactic tradition: 'I was like a gleaner,' he says, 'following the grape-pickers.'[2] His work might easily be disregarded as presenting much too late a development to illuminate the training of scribes in Solomon's Jerusalem, were it not for the remarkable conservatism of its teaching and, in particular, its quite obvious continuity with the tradition of scribal education in Egypt.

The 'wisdom' of which Ben Sira was a professional and experienced teacher was what he himself called 'the theory and art of serving the great'.[3] Like his Egyptian predecessors, he trained his pupils for success in their careers by trying to inculcate habits of clear thinking,[4] persuasive speech,[5] and judicious timing,[6] although it is evident that his efforts were often frustrated:

> Teaching a fool is like mending pottery with glue . . .
> Prepare what you have to say, if you want a hearing;
> marshal your learning and then give your answer.
> The feelings of a fool turn like a cart-wheel,
> and his thoughts spin like an axle.[7]

As in the Egyptian scribal schools, Ben Sira's responsibilities embraced those of a 'moral tutor', and we find him not only uttering conventional warnings about wine, women and gossip,[8] but giving avuncular advice about dining with a prospective employer ('under cover of geniality he will be weighing you up'[9]), good manners at banquets,[10] living on credit,[11] and the great advantages of a stable family life.[12]

His preoccupation with popularity and promotion, like his strictures on the dangers of social-climbing, reflect a mobile and meritocratic community and imply that many of his pupils were boys of humble origin and modest means:

> Do not lift a weight too heavy for you,
> keeping company with a man greater and richer than yourself.
> How can a jug be friends with a kettle?
> If they knock together, the one will be smashed.[13]

For Ben Sira, no less than for his Egyptian prototypes, education for the public service was as broad as it was long and included, therefore, instruction in religion and morals. Although he was an admirer of the High Priest,[14] an enthusiastic adherent of the Established Religion and a devoted exponent of the Law of Moses,[15] his personal religion was deeply indebted to the simple and emphatically moral piety which is found in the educational manuals of Egypt.[16] Ben Sira interpreted the whole of experience – from the order of nature to his personal fortunes[17] – as the plan ordained by a benevolent Providence, to be accepted without question:

> All men alike come from the ground;
> Adam was created out of the earth.
> Yet in his great wisdom the Lord distinguished them
> and made them go various ways;
> some he blessed and lifted high,
> some he hallowed and brought near to himself,
> some he cursed and humbled
> and removed from their place.
> As clay is in the potter's hands,
> to be moulded just as he chooses,
> so are men in the hands of their Maker,
> to be dealt with as he decides.[18]

Strangely, however, this conservative passivity is balanced by a sturdy emphasis on man's independence and responsibility. Ben Sira taught his pupils that they must be self-reliant, make their own decisions, and be active in promoting the welfare of those who suffer misfortune.[19] In this respect, too, he is a late heir to the paradoxical teaching of the Egyptian scribal schools.[20]

THE EGYPTIAN SCRIBAL SCHOOLS

Among the many constantly recurring themes in this extraordinarily stable tradition of teaching, none is more illuminating than the satirical contrast between the wretched lot of the manual worker and the luxurious and influential life of the scribe. Ben Sira's version of it is the latest and most familiar:[21]

> A scholar's wisdom comes of ample leisure;
> if a man is to be wise he must be relieved of other tasks.
> How can a man become wise who guides the plough,
> whose pride is in wielding his goad,
> who is absorbed in the task of driving oxen,
> and talks only about cattle?
> He concentrates on ploughing his furrows,
> and works late to give the heifers their fodder.

Ben Sira's list of undesirable jobs goes on to those of the engraver of signets, the ironworker and the potter, who, though necessary to 'maintain the fabric of this world', lack the education to take any significant part in public affairs. Not so the scribe:

> How different it is with the man who devotes himself
> to studying the law of the Most High,
> who investigates all the wisdom of the past,
> and spends his time studying the prophecies!
> He preserves the sayings of famous men
> and penetrates the intricacies of parables.
> He investigates the hidden meaning of proverbs
> and knows his way among riddles.

> The great avail themselves of his services,
> and he is seen in the presence of rulers.
> He travels in foreign countries
> and learns at first hand the good or evil of man's lot.

Although Ben Sira's ideal scribe is now a student of the scriptures, he is still engaged in government service, as were the scribes of Egypt from the third millennium BC and, indeed, as were most men of learning until the expansion and professionalizing of university education in the last hundred years. Ben Sira's explicit recognition that craftsmen possess their own peculiar dignity and that manual labour and farm work are not to be despised[22] has led to the suggestion that he was influenced by later and more democratic versions of the classical Egyptian tradition,[23] such as the *Instructions of Onchsheshonqy*, written, perhaps, some two centuries before Ecclesiasticus, and clearly addressed to a modest farming community ('Let your son learn to write, to plough, to fowl and to trap according to the season of the year').[24] However, this rural background is wholly exceptional in the Egyptian material known to us, and it remains probable that Ben Sira, who is more familiar with the corridors of power than the furrows of the field, was primarily indebted to the earlier Egyptian school books.

In the Egyptian schools of the Ramesside period, the most popular of all the text-books, to judge by the fact that over seventy copies of it have so far come to light,[25] was a mocking caricature of the 'cloth-cap' world of the working man, commonly called the *Satire of the Trades*,[26] written by a scribe named Khety, son of Duauf, about 1960 BC. Khety purports to be offering advice to his son as he was sailing up the Nile to join the State Secretarial School at Memphis, where the government of the time was making a great effort to recruit candidates for the civil service.[27] The body of this work consists of seventeen paragraphs, each depicting in the liveliest detail the horrors of being a particular kind of manual worker – a smith, carpenter, engraver, barber, merchant,

Fig. 21 Painting from the tomb of Ammenemes I at Beni Hasan (Dynasty XII). From top to bottom, it depicts (a) makers of knives and sandals; (b) makers of bows, arrows, barrels, chairs and boxes; (c) goldsmiths; (d) potters; (e) flax and linen workers; (f) harvesters; (g) farmers ploughing and sowing.

building-contractor, stonemason, market-gardener, tenant farmer, weaver, arrow-maker, courier, embalmer, cobbler, laundryman, bird-catcher and fisherman, all catalogued in order to bring home the obvious moral: 'Behold, there is no profession free of a boss – except for the scribe: *he is the boss.*'

It was, one hopes, the caustic humour of this piece, rather than its smug superiority, which made it the favourite writing exercise of Egyptian schoolboys and the model for many imitators in the period preceding the age of Solomon. For example, the Papyrus Lansing,[28] an instruction in letter-writing 'made by the royal scribe and chief overseer of cattle . . . for his apprentice', is almost entirely monopolized by this theme of the superiority of the scribe's life. 'Love writing,' the master counsels, 'hate pleasure, that you may be a worthy magistrate. Do not give your heart to the covert; neglect throwing the boomerang and bouncing. Spend the whole day writing with your fingers, whilst you read by night. Take as your friends the papyrus-roll and the palette. . . .' The advice, apparently, was expected to fall on deaf ears, since the pupil was required to continue in his copying: 'You are too busy going in and out, unmindful of writing. You have . . . neglected my teachings. You are worse than the Nile-goose of the river-bank, that abounds in mischief.' He had better consider, therefore, the ghastly alternatives to graduating as a proficient scribe:

Look for yourself with your own eye. The professions are set before you. The *washerman* spends the whole day going up and down, all his body is weak through whitening the clothes of his neighbours every day and washing their linen. The *potter* is smeared with earth like a person one of whose folk has died. His hands and his feet are full of clay. . . . The *sandal-maker* mixes tan; his odour is conspicuous. . . . The *merchants* fare downstream and upstream, and are as busy as brass, carrying goods from one town to another. . . . The *ships' crews* of every commercial house have received their loads so that they may depart from Egypt to Djahy [Palestine and Phoenicia]. Each man's god is with him. Not one of them dares say: 'We shall see Egypt again.' A *carpenter*, the one who is in the ship-yard, carries the timber and stacks it. If he renders today his produce of yesterday, woe to his limbs! The shipwright stands behind him to say to him evil things. His *outworker* who is in the fields, *that* is tougher than any profession. He spends the whole day laden with his tools, tied down to his tool-box. He goes back to his house in the evening laden with the tool-box and the timber, his drinking mug and his whetstones. *But the scribe, it is he that reckons the produce of all those. Take note of this.*

Two new categories of work enter the school satire of the Ramesside period – those of the farmer and soldier – and both are scorned in this royal scribe's text-book. 'Let me explain to you,' he writes,

the condition of the cultivator, that other hard profession. . . . He spends the day cutting implements for cultivating corn. He spends the night twisting rope. . . . He spends time cultivating corn regularly, but the snake is after him, and finishes off the seed-corn when cast to the ground. He sees not a green blade. He does it with three sowings of borrowed barley. His wife has fallen to the lot of merchants, and found no advantage in exchange. Now the scribe has landed at the river-bank. He registers the harvest-tax, apparitors being after him with staffs. . . . One says: 'Give corn!', and there is none. He is beaten furiously. He is bound and thrown into the well; he is soused in a headlong dipping, his wife having been bound in his presence. His children are in fetters. His neighbours abandon them and are fled. It's all up! No corn! *If you have any sense, be a scribe.*

The master's warning about becoming a soldier is particularly interesting for the impression it gives of Palestine and for its introductory account of his pupil's prospects as a scribe:

Behold, I am teaching you and making sound your body to enable you to hold the palette freely, to cause you to become a trusty one of the king, to cause you to open treasuries and granaries, to cause you to receive [corn] from the ship at the entrance of the granary, and to cause you to issue the divine offerings on festal days, attired in fine raiment, with horses, whilst your bark is on the Nile, and you are provided with apparitors, moving freely and inspecting. A villa has been built in your city, and you hold a powerful office, by the king's gift to you. Male and female slaves are in your neighbourhood, and those who are in the fields in holdings of your own making will grasp your hand. . . . Put writing in your heart that you may protect yourself from all manner of toil and be a worthy magistrate. . . . Come, let me describe to you the woes of a soldier. . . . He is called up for Khor [Syria–Palestine], and he does not spare himself. There are no clothes and no sandals. . . . During his long marchings on the hills he drinks water every three days, and it is smelly and tastes like salt. His body is broken with dysentery. The enemy is come and surrounds him with arrows. . . . His body is weak and his knee is feeble on account of him [i.e. the enemy]. The victory is attained, and the captives and tribespeople destined to Egypt are handed over to His Majesty. The foreign woman has fainted through marching and is placed upon the soldier's neck. His haversack is dropped, and others take it away, as he is loaded with a captive-woman. His wife and children are now in their village; he is dead, he has not reached it. If he comes out as a survivor he is weak with marching. Whether he is at large or whether he is in captivity, the soldier is vexed. He is fled and gone away amongst the deserters, whilst all his folk are confined in jail. Now he is dead upon the desert-edges, and there is no one to perpetuate his name. . . . *Be a scribe*, that you may be saved from being a soldier; that you may call out and one may say: 'Here am I'; that you may be delivered from torments. Everyone seeks to uplift him. Take note of this.

The class-room correspondence of the Papyrus Lansing ends with the pupil's ingratiating declaration that he intends to build a new villa for his master and an effusive eulogy of the royal scribe's splendid participation in religious ceremonies, in addition to his skill and success as an administrator.[29]

It is extraordinary that men as devoted to learning as the scribes of Egypt should have made so few explicit references to their schools and educational system. This reticence ought to encourage Old Testament scholars not to interpret the silence of their own documents in the usual negative way. Both in Egypt and in Israel, the best evidence for scribal education is its literary fruits and the existence of a complex bureaucracy, but a little more detail may be gleaned from the less formal writings which have survived in the dry climate of Egypt.[30]

In the Ramesside period, which best illuminates the Egyptian context of Israel's emergence as a nation, schools were attached to the great state institutions – the Temples, the Treasury and the Army – and large caches of writing exercises on ostraca at particular places suggest the use of recognized school buildings.[31] The admissions policy of these

29 Painting of a banqueting scene in the Theban tomb of a scribe employed by a temple official in the reign of Tuthmosis IV (Dynasty XVIII). From left to right, a woman plays a harp covered with leopard skin; she is followed by a nude lutanist and a little girl dancing. The player of the double pipes looks back towards a woman plucking a lyre with a plectrum.

30 Fragment of an ivory ointment box (height 6 cm.) from Nimrud (8th century BC). It depicts royal musicians, men and women, playing the lyre, drum and flute. The men wear heavy Egyptian or Phoenician wigs and the background consists of voluted palmettes.

31 Fragment of a painting on a Cairo papyrus (Dynasty XX–XXI). The artist mocks the foibles of men by representing them in the guise of animals. A cat is shown dressing a mouse, who is elegantly attired as a lady of the court, sitting on a wicker stool and holding a glass of wine. A cat follows nursing a baby mouse. On the right, foxes are shown in the reversed role of feeding cattle.

32 Relief in the tomb of Ay at Amarna (Dynasty XVIII). Akhenaten, Nefertiti and three of their daughters are seen in the Palace Window of Appearances as they present gifts to Ay, Master of the Horse, and his wife Tey.

33 Painting from the Theban tomb of Menna, 'Scribe of the fields of the Lord of the Two Lands' (Dynasty XVIII). He is shown in a papyrus shelter supervising his scribes' registration of the harvest.

state schools was by no means socially exclusive. For example, the craftsmen of Deir el-Medina, working on the Theban necropolis, were taught to read and write; similarly, the boy for whom the *Instruction of Ani* is supposed to have been written was the son of a modest temple-scribe and during his time at school it was his own mother who provided his meals: 'She put thee into school when thou were taught to write, and she continued on thy behalf every day, with bread and beer in her house.'[32]

A potential scribe probably entered the Junior School at the age of five and began his instruction in writing by reproducing hieroglyphic signs as 'pictures'. In the Middle School, he started the study of hieratic, the cursive script which had developed naturally from hieroglyphic for everyday use. The teaching method at this second stage seems to have been supremely cautious and conventional – as in the days when English children learned to write 'copper plate' from copybooks. The pupil copied extracts from a standard text and reproduced to the last detail what he had before his eyes. Fascinating evidence of this tedious occupation came to light recently with the discovery of the so-called *Book of Kemit*, a collection of advice about hard work and self-control, composed about 1960 BC but still widely used in the Ramesside period.[33] The Ramesside ostraca giving selections from it disclose that pupils were made to reproduce the more formal hieratic script of the 'classical' age in which it was originally composed, and even arrange the text in vertical columns, despite the fact that this method had been generally abandoned in favour of horizontal writing some centuries earlier. The absence of any signs of individuality in these exercises makes it fairly clear that pupils copied mechanically without much attempt to understand what it was they were writing.

In the Senior School, young men were at last free to branch out into 'modern studies', which meant that they began to use recent texts written in the vernacular and to copy model 'business' letters devised by their masters, like those in the Papyrus Lansing. Although a few ancient works, like the *Story of Sinuhe*,[34] were still part of the syllabus, the study of the classics seems to have declined in the Ramesside period and, with it, intellectual standards generally. Egyptologists lament the carelessness with which texts were copied, and since the exercises in the vernacular are as riddled with errors as those from the classics, the obscurity of Middle Egyptian cannot be pleaded as an excuse. The adoption of dictation and memorizing as teaching methods may have contributed to this deterioration, but one suspects that most of the students (and many of their tutors) were more interested in careers than in learning for its own sake. The school texts often emphasize that education is a means to an end:

I have placed you at school along with the children of magistrates in order to instruct and to teach you concerning this aggrandizing calling. Look, I tell you the way of the scribe in his [perpetual] 'Early to your place! Write in front of your companions! Lay your hand on your clothes and attend to your sandals!' You bring your book daily with a purpose, be not idle. They say 'Three plus three'. . . . You will make calculations quietly: let no sound from your mouth be heard. Write with your hand, read with your mouth, and take advice. Be not weary, spend no day of idleness, or woe to your limbs! Fall in with the ways of your instructor and hear his teachings. *Be a scribe*.[35]

The reference in this letter to elementary arithmetic indicates how the syllabus of modern studies was geared to practical ends. The Egyptian bureaucrats' passion for inventories and book-keeping presupposes some training in figures and their laborious methods of calculation are known to us from two documents of the Middle Kingdom (2050–1786 BC) – the Moscow Papyrus and the Rhind Mathematical Papyrus.[36] Modern studies also included geography – the kind which a potential provincial administrator or diplomatic representative would need to know. How the subject was taught is clearly illustrated by the *Satirical Letter* of Hori, written, probably, in the reign of Ramesses II, and a firm favourite of schoolmasters throughout the Ramesside period.[37]

This lively document takes the form of a reply by Hori, a scribe who contrived to combine the posts of 'teacher of apprentices in the Office of Writings' and 'Groom of His Majesty', to a letter received from Amenemope, a scribe on active service as an army commander in Syria and Palestine. The writer has a gift for caricature and uses it to deflate the kind of nit-wit who grows too big for his boots when posted abroad. Amenemope pretends to deep scribal learning, ponderously quoting ancient authorities (without any knowledge of the primary source): 'I am more profound as a scribe than heaven or earth or the underworld. I know the mountains in *deben* and *hin* [weights and measures]'.[38] Above all, he claims to be a *mahir*, a title of uncertain derivation which probably meant a military scribe experienced in foreign travel who could be used on missions abroad.[39]

Amenemope's pretensions cannot, however, conceal his incompetence. On this peg, Hori hangs a number of model lessons for his scribal students – in letter-writing, arithmetic and geography. In the last section of the letter, Amenemope is subjected to a class-room grilling on his knowledge of the region from northern Syria to the Egyptian frontier: 'Let me tell thee of another strange city, named Byblos. What is it like? And its goddess? Once again – thou hast not trodden it. Pray, instruct me about Beirut, about Sidon and Sarepta. Where is the stream of the Litani? What is Uzu like?' And so on, for pages.[40] In addition to its claims as an early Baedeker, Hori's letter reveals a smattering of foreign languages and a certain flair for descriptive writing such as is common to Egyptian compositions and the biblical literature of Solomon's age:

Thy letter reached me in an hour of relaxing for a while. I found thy message as I was sitting beside the horse which is in my charge. I rejoiced and was glad and ready to answer. When I went into my stall to look at thy letter, I found that it was neither praises nor insults. Thy statements mix up this with that; all thy words are upside down; they are not connected. . . .[41]

Hori was clearly an able man and the schools which used his letter as a text-book must have been more than treadmill secretarial colleges.

One of the ways in which Hori showed his ability was the skill with which he animated the deadly dull lists of persons, places and things then circulating in the scribal schools. Of these, the *Onomasticon of Amenope*, written about 1085 BC, is the most exhaustive:

Beginning of the teaching for clearing the mind, for instruction of the ignorant and for learning all things that exist: what Ptah created, what Thoth copied down, heaven with its affairs, earth and what is in it, what the mountains belch forth, what is watered by the flood, all things upon which Re has shone, all that is grown on the back of earth, excogitated by the scribe of the sacred books in the House of Life, Amenope.⁴²

The scribe then proceeds to list some 610 'things'; 1–62, Sky, water, earth; 63–229, Persons, court, offices, occupations; 230–312, Classes, tribes, and types of human being; 313–419, The towns of Egypt; 420–73, Buildings, their parts, and types of land; 474–555, Agricultural land, cereals and their products; 556–78, Beverages; 579–610, Parts of an ox and kinds of meat.⁴³ Such encyclopedic knowledge, listed in order, immediately recalls the 'wisdom' of Solomon: 'He discoursed of trees, *from* the cedar of Lebanon *down to* the marjoram that grows out of the wall, of beasts and birds, of reptiles and fishes.'⁴⁴ It is reasonable to speculate that *onomastica* were as familiar to the scribes of Solomon's court as they were to Hori, since, even if the *Onomasticon of Amenope* in the unfinished form we now have it contains no references to trees, plants, beasts, birds, reptiles and fish, the older 'Ramesseum Onomasticon' (*c.* 1786–1633 BC) does.⁴⁵ If, as seems probable, later Old Testament literature is indebted to the use of these *onomastica* in scribal schools (including the hectoring speech in which God deflates Job, as mercilessly as Hori deflates Amenemope), it is even more likely that the Egyptian models were influential in the early years of the monarchy.⁴⁶

Fig. 22   Painting from the Theban tomb of Nefer-hotep (Dynasty XVIII). Nefer-hotep, chief scribe of Amun and superintendent of oxen and heifers, is shown with his wife offering worship to the deified king Amenophis I. He presents a bird and a loaf on a brazier.

Lists of officials and occupations, like those given in the *onomastica*, left the student-scribe in no doubt about the wealth of lucrative careers open to men of education. They display the whole range from Vizier to the Preparer of Tripe and include such attractive-sounding posts as that of the 'Chief of the record-keepers of the House of the Great Green' (i.e. the Mediterranean). It was, however, only in the multifarious branches of government institutions that promising jobs were available; there is no evidence of any 'private sector'.[47] As the scribal schools were attached to these state departments, there was no sharp dividing line between pupil and employee such as a school-leaving age represents, and it would appear that junior apprentices continued their education under senior officials. 'The Pharaonic writers', a distinguished Egyptologist once observed, 'held the laudable view that a man is never too old to learn, together with the perhaps less laudable view that one is never too old to teach.' The Ramesside letters certainly show a great variety of established civil servants (like Hori, the Royal Groom) actively engaged in further education.[48] Their avuncular attitude is well illustrated in a document which must rank as the first-recorded prototype of the School Speech Day Address by a distinguished Old Boy:

Although I have seen many like you who were in a chamber of writings and did not fail to swear by God that they would never write, they did become scribes and their names were found fit to send them on missions. *And you have seen me myself.* When I was of your age I spent my life in the stocks: it was they that tamed my limbs. They stayed three months with me. I was imprisoned in the temple whilst my father and mother were in the field as well as my brothers and sisters. They left me only after my hand was deft and I had surpassed whoever was in front of me, I being the first amongst all my companions, having surpassed them in books. Do as I have said, that your body may be sound and you may be found tomorrow having no superiors.[49]

Ancient Egypt never entertained the myth that government and administration are best left in the hands of amateurs and so it showed no gentlemanly inhibitions about revealing explicitly the expertise – the 'wisdom' – needed for their successful execution. Manuals of instruction were produced to teach the young man how to make a success of his future career, whether he was destined to follow his father in some important hereditary office, or whether he was seeking a modest post (with prospects) in the labyrinth of the Pharaoh's vast bureaucracy. These 'guide books to success' sought to communicate the fruits of past experience not only on such professional matters as man-management and public-speaking, but also on the kind of personal conduct which helped or hindered a man's progress in life. That such counsel was not as calculating and prudential as at first appears is clear from the earliest example of this genre to have survived intact – the *Instruction of Ptahhotep.*[50]

The 'Instruction of Ptahhotep'

Written about 2350 B C, this brief work breathes the stability and serenity of the Old Kingdom. It takes the form of an address by an aged vizier to his son and successor, but, whatever its actual origin, the text was handed down the centuries as an educational manual for use in the training of an élite for high office in the State. As recently discovered ostraca show, it was still current as a classic in the schools of the Ramesside period. The basic counsel given to the candidate for government service is that he should make himself an agent of *ma 'at*, that cosmic order which found expression in the divine kingship of the Pharaoh and derivatively in the just ordering of society:

If thou art a leader commanding the affairs of the multitude, seek out for thyself every beneficial deed, until it may be that thy own affairs are without wrong. Justice (*ma 'at*) is great, and its appropriateness is lasting; it has not been disturbed since the time of him who made it, whereas there is punishment for him who passes over its laws.

Although this fundamental concept undermines the temptation to arrogance and ambitious self-assertion – for success is a divine gift – it positively demands a serious and intelligent grasp of past tradition, for 'there is no one born wise'. A candidate for high office must, therefore, acquire knowledge of 'the rules for good speech' (when and, especially, when *not* to voice an opinion), the rules for acting as an envoy, the rules for maintaining harmony in social relations, and the rules for dealing with petitioners: 'Be calm as thou listenest to the petitioner's speech. . . . A petitioner likes attention to his words better than the fulfilling of that for which he came.' Since a public man's private life affects not only his own career, but his wider social obligations, he is counselled to establish a stable home and love his wife 'as is fitting', be rigorous in the discipline of his sons, avoid family feuds and shun sexual promiscuity. It is prudent as well as just for an official to share his wealth with his subordinates and proper to accept calmly the success of the *nouveaux-riches*. Since 'it is god who makes a man's quality', you cannot elbow your way to the top. Ptahhotep's basic conviction that all is determined by a Divine Order has the admirable effect of engendering tranquillity without destroying initiative.

THE 'INSTRUCTION OF ANI'

The confidence of Ptahhotep is no longer to be found in the educational manuals of the Ramesside era, largely, it seems, because they derive from more modest members of a society which had itself become less assured. The *Instruction of Ani*,[51] written by a temple-scribe allegedly for his son, reflects the hopes and fears of aspirants to middle-class status and breathes an atmosphere of suburban domesticity far removed from the centre of power and the grandeur of life at court. It is addressed to schoolboys from homes which have gardens but no servants, where the mother of the family nurses her own babies, takes the children's lunch to school, does all the housework and is said to deserve a husband who will give her a helping hand. With a view to their career as scribes, the boys from this background must learn to keep things to them-selves ('Do not talk a lot. Be silent, and thou wilt be happy'), to be careful about the friends they make, to avoid women and drink, to be respectful to superiors and not answer them back, to keep on good terms with the police and not get mixed up in demonstrations, and, above all, to grasp the golden opportunities afforded by scribal education: 'Devote thyself to the writings, and put them in thine heart, and then all that thou sayest is excellent. To whatsoever office the scribe is appointed, he consulteth the writings.' Ani is no more motivated by Ptahhotep's *ma 'at* than the twentieth-century railway clerk by Kant's Categorical Imperative. He recognizes, indeed, a transcendent power, which governs all things, bringing the rich to poverty and the young to death, but the gap between this impersonal concept and his actual existence has now been filled by a personal god who cares: 'Pray thou with a loving heart, all the words of which are

Fig. 23   Painting from the Theban tomb of Nefer-hotep (Dynasty XVIII). The superintendent scribe is seated as he dictates to two clerks, each with a palette and an unrolled sheet of papyrus.

hidden, and he will do what thou needest, he will hear what thou sayest, and he will accept thy offering.'

THE 'INSTRUCTION OF AMENEMOPE'

The explicitly religious bias of scribal education in the Ramesside period is further illustrated by the *Instruction of Amenemope*,[52] written sometime before 1000 BC by an administrator in the Ministry of Agriculture. This Amenemope is not, of course, to be confused with the scribe who was the butt of Hori's satire. For him, as for the Hebrew prophet Isaiah,[53] wisdom consists in the calm acceptance of what has been divinely ordained. It is useless for a man to join in the rat-race – to 'strain' and 'push',[54] since everything has been determined by Fate and Fortune;[55] even *ma 'at* is a gift of God and subject to his will.[56] Success comes by committing oneself silently into God's hands and leaving the issue to be decided according to his 'plan'.[57] Even opponents are to be dealt with in a spirit of serenity and trust:

> Do not say: 'I have found a strong superior,
> For a man in thy city has injured me.'
> Do not say: 'I have found a patron,
> For one who hates me has injured me.'

> For surely thou knowest not the plans of god,
> Lest thou be ashamed on the morrow.
> Sit thou down at the hands of the god,
> And thy silence will cast them down.[58]

Thomas à Kempis based his maxim *Homo proponit sed Deus disponit* on aphorisms from the book of Proverbs, but these were directly derived from this central concept of Amenemope's teaching:

> One thing are the words which men say,
> Another is that which god does . . .
> If the tongue of a man [be] the rudder of a boat,
> The All-Lord is its pilot.[59]

God is equally the sole ground of morality – 'it is sealed with his finger'.[60] He 'determines the boundaries of the arable land',[61] upholds honesty in buying and selling,[62] abominates false talk and false records[63] and brings retribution on all who flout his will.[64] The moral life consists, therefore, neither in promoting the harmony of society, nor in actualizing an abstract Cosmic Order, but in doing the will of God. He is man's creator and that is the reason for acting with compassion towards the needy:

> Do not laugh at a blind man nor tease a dwarf
> Nor injure the affairs of the lame.
> Do not tease a man who is in the hand of the god [i.e. insane],
> Nor be fierce of face against him if he errs.
> For man is clay and straw,
> And the god is his builder.[65]

It is because 'God desires respect for the poor more than the honouring of the exalted' that a man should care for the widow and stranger[66] and deal generously with the poor debtor as did the Dishonest Steward, who was commended for his prudence in the Lucan parable:

> If thou findest a large debt against a poor man,
> Make it into three parts,
> Forgive two, and let one stand.

Thou will find it like the ways of life;
Thou wilt lie down and sleep soundly; in the morning
Thou wilt find it again like good news.[67]

Such was the religious and moral context in which Amenemope sought to train the grammar-school boy for a successful career in the civil service.[68] He should aim to become 'the
truly silent man'[69] – reticent,[70] tactful,[71] imperturbable,[72]
unambitious,[73] self-effacing,[74] reliable,[75] just[76] and scrupu-
lously honest.[77] He should avoid currying favour with the
great[78] and be content with that station in life to which it had
pleased God to call him.[79]

THE BOOK OF PROVERBS
The *Instruction of Amenemope* is particularly interesting as the
principal source of a section of the biblical book of Proverbs
(22.17–23.14), in which the Israelite scribe has often adopted
the Egyptian text *verbatim*.[80] This explicit connection, recognized for nearly half a century, has only recently been
acknowledged as a significant clue to the background of
Solomon's new bureaucracy. The reluctance of Old Testament scholars to find in the book of Proverbs an Israelite
counterpart of the Egyptian instruction, similarly designed
for the education of scribes, is largely due to the conviction
that in so far as its material is early it derives from popular
tradition, and in so far as it is presented in a structured literary
form, or with an explicitly theological motivation, it must
have passed through the hands of later Jewish editors. None
of these pillars of critical orthodoxy is firmly based. In the
first place, the book of Proverbs is not really a book of
proverbs, since its aphorisms are obviously not distillations of
popular wisdom in that characteristically concrete but allu-
sive style which teases the imagination ('When a crocodile
surfaces, its length is measured'), but, rather, contrived
literary sentences couched in somewhat flat language, employing simile and metaphor to limit instead of extend their
range of meaning ('A king's rage is like a lion's roar, his
favour like dew on the grass').[81] It appears, therefore, that

this misnamed 'proverbial' material, generally regarded as the earliest element in the book, is the work of educated and consciously literary men. Secondly, most of the structured complexes to be found in chapters 1–9, generally regarded as the latest section of the book, are probably not the end-product of a long literary development which built up larger units from single sentences, but, rather, passages of 'instruction', characterized by the use of the imperative and a direct, unadorned style, parallel to the sections borrowed from the *Instruction of Amenemope*.[82] The form of this material is plainly didactic and, as such, it does not demand a date later than the age of Solomon.[83] Thirdly, the theological motivation of the book does not necessarily indicate a prolonged process of development from the basic Egyptian models. Even the ancient *Instruction of Ptahhotep* gives its guidance for top-level statesmanship in a quasi-theological context and the school manuals for the training of ordinary civil servants written during the Ramesside period – the *Instruction of Ani* and the *Instruction of Amenemope* – are even more positively religious than their Israelite counterpart. The view that Egyptian scribes were trained in a hard-headed pragmatic school, which left them free to make empirical judgments without reference to any moral or religious criteria, and that this intellectually rigorous and secular outlook came to be undermined in Israel by religious morality and dogmatic piety owes more to the rationalistic prejudices of those who hold it than to the available evidence.

It is not the contrast but the common ground between the book of Proverbs and the Egyptian Instructions which emerges as the significant feature. In adopting the Egyptian educational material for use in Israel, it is surprising that the scribes of Jerusalem were satisfied with such slight modifications. We search the book of Proverbs in vain for any reference to Israel's distinctive belief in God's self-revelation in history, prophecy or law,[84] and the only cultic prescription included in the work,[85] like the sentences which subordinate sacrifice to morality,[86] is paralleled in the Egyptian scribal

tradition. The theology of the book of Proverbs (allowing
for the substitution of Yahweh for the many gods – or the
God of many names – of Egypt) is more or less identical with
that which was taught to the candidates for the Pharaoh's
civil service. The world is ordered by the providence of the
Creator,[87] to whose bounty man should respond in quiet
faith[88] and humble piety.[89] The issue of all things is in his
hands,[90] but divine grace does not annihilate human freedom.[91] Those who walk in the way of righteousness receive
blessing and long life, while the wicked are brought to
judgment and death.[92] God is the arbiter of right and wrong[93]
and demands justice in the law courts,[94] honest dealing in the
market-place,[95] and generosity to the poor,[96] since they are
no less his creatures than the rich and powerful.[97] The man of
God does not repay evil for evil, but conquers it by kindness.[98]

It would be hazardous to assert that the whole of the book
of Proverbs was composed in the early years of the Israelite
monarchy, but the bulk of its material is so close to the late
Egyptian scribal tradition in both form and content that
there is no reason to doubt its explicit claim to have origina-
ted in the age of Solomon.[99] Further, it represents the work of
men who had received a scribal education and affords the
most direct evidence we possess for the school or schools
which Solomon must have established in order to train
candidates for his new bureaucracy. It is impossible to be
confident about the book's precise relationship to this training
and attempts to identify within it texts designed for use in the
class-room are inevitably somewhat arbitrary.[100] The fact
that the Egyptian instructions included guidance for life as
well as for scribal careers should, at least, warn us against
concluding that the book of Proverbs is far too general to
have formed part of the syllabus of King's College, Jerusalem. Solomon's teachers had the task of creating a class of
'new men' previously unknown in Israel and the type by
whom and for whom the book of Proverbs was largely
written is entirely credible in the context of the emergent
nation. This new man merits closer inspection.

THE NEW MAN OF PROVERBS

The man of Proverbs is a highly-motivated member of the lower middle class. He 'makes straight for his goal'[101] and that goal is disclosed in his two favourite mottoes: 'Be timid in business and come to beggary; be bold and make a fortune';[102] 'Diligence brings a man to power'.[103] He identifies himself neither with the rich nor yet with the poor,[104] is determined to 'have nothing to do with men of rank',[105] and disapproves when men of different stations pretend to be what they are not.[106] Although he is fully aware that 'the road of the diligent is a highway',[107] he has no intention of trying to get rich quick;[108] from the folly of speculators he has learnt the lesson that 'wealth quickly come by dwindles away, but if it comes little by little, it multiplies'.[109] He has always steered clear of the credit rackets of the commercial world and never got trapped into standing surety for money-lenders' advances to unreliable foreigners.[110] He knows that money is not the be-all and end-all of life and he wants to get his priorities right.[111] What is more, he has his home and family to think about,[112] even though he is ambitious to give them security[113] and 'all the precious and pleasant things that wealth can buy'.[114]

He is, as the saying goes,[115] very much a 'home-bird', backed up by a devoted and extremely capable wife. Not only does she see to the meals and the children's clothes, but works all hours to earn a bit extra.[116] A wife, he holds, makes a world of difference to a man in his position.[117] He is one who sets great store by domestic peace and feels sorry for men with 'a nagging wife and a brawling household',[118] where the sons are always contradicting their father and getting their mother upset.[119] He always says that it is important to 'start a boy on the right road',[120] especially now, when it is education and not birth which counts.[121] In these days, when you can choose a career,[122] there's no point in ending up as a labourer.[123] That is why he believes in being strict with his boys and knocking some sense into them.[124] He was brought up to accept parental authority himself[125] and that is the way it ought to be,[126] especially when it is easier than ever it was for a lad to get in with a bunch of crooks or a boozing crowd,[127] and the streets are swarming with women on the loose,[128] some of them rich and exotic, with their husbands away on business.[129] If he fails to watch his step,[130] a young man with prospects can quickly wreck his career.[131] It does not follow, of course, that you should keep yourself to yourself;[132] a family certainly needs friends[133] – the sort you can drop in on (within reason, of course)[134] and say just what you think,[135] as distinct from casual acquaintances or mere hangers-on.[136] It is enjoyable to have friends in to a meal – nothing elaborate, but intimate and relaxed, with none of the glittering hypocrisy of those formal dinner parties.[137]

The man of Proverbs is an open, cheerful character,[138] who speaks his mind[139] and does everything in his power to promote neighbourliness in the community at large.[140] He hates gossiping of every kind[141] and especially all the quarrels it sparks off.[142] The way to deal with enemies, he believes, is not by revenge but by the same sort of generosity[143] a man ought to show to everybody in need.[144] He would not want to deny that he has his principles, but he prefers to think of himself as a practical man, for whom getting results is all-important,[145] even if sometimes it does mean compromise. There are occasions, for example, when a bribe works 'like a charm'[146] and to turn a blind eye is the only sensible thing to do.[147]

Such realism is the secret of his success. He has learnt how to handle men and win their co-operation. The essence of his method is to play it by ear and to play it cool[148] and this demands complete self-control and infinite patience.[149] As something of an expert in group dynamics, he knows that a heated debate is no substitute for a rational discussion.[150] In the former, self-opinionated hot-heads talk contentiously and too much;[151] in the latter, progress is made by genuine dialogue, in which discerning men elicit each other's views, as water is drawn from the depths of a well,[152] and sharpen each other's wits 'as iron sharpens iron'.[153] In such discussions, it is vital to conceal your feelings,[154] to hear a question out before attempting an answer,[155] and to make your own contribution at the right moment[156] and in the right words.[157] Decisions should never be taken in a hurry;[158] they demand the weighing of evidence[159] and careful thought.[160] What counts in the end is the 'know-how' which is born of experience[161] and the rigorous use of a carefully-trained mind.[162]

Men of this kind were needed in large numbers to keep the wheels turning in Solomon's emergent nation and the scribal teachers of Jerusalem were charged with the task of producing them. For those who were prepared to learn what was expected of them,[163] respect authority[164] and work hard,[165] there were openings in plenty and for the really ambitious Room at the Top.[166]

34 Detail from a relief in the tomb of Khaemhet (Dynasty XVIII). It shows two young scribes with carefully dressed hair and fine thin garments holding papyrus rolls recording the cattle in their charge.

35 Statue in black serpentine or steatite (height 14 cm.) from Amarna in the later reign of Akhenaten (Dynasty XVIII). It depicts a scribe, who probably commissioned the work, squatting characteristically and writing under the inspiration of Thoth, the god of learning, here represented by his ape, crowned with the disc and crescent of the moon.

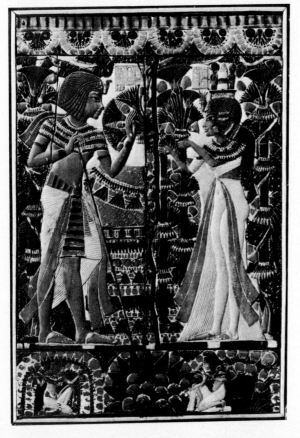

36 Painting from the Theban tomb of Ipy, a sculptor in the reign of Ramesses II (Dynasty XIX). The peripteral chapel reflects a style going back to the beginning of Dynasty XVIII. The irrigation of the garden and the dog behind the gardener are beautifully observed.

37 Panel from a casket-lid on a veneer of ivory (22 × 32 cm.) depicting Tutankhamun and his queen, Ankhesenamun (Dynasty XVIII). As they stand in their bower, the queen is offering the king a bouquet of flowers and mandrake fruits, or love-apples.

CHAPTER SIX

The literature of the scribes

IT IS NOW generally agreed that the literary enterprise we know as the Old Testament was launched during Israel's dramatic emergence as a nation under David and Solomon. The 'Succession Story' or 'Court History of David' (II Samuel 9–20, with I Kings 1, 2) and the Yahwist's history of Israel, tracing the people's destiny from the Creation of the World to the Conquest of Palestine, have for long been praised as remarkable literary and intellectual achievements. It is only comparatively recently, however, that scholars have sought to explain how and why an unsophisticated people like Israel quite suddenly began to produce works of such outstanding merit. This newly-awakened enquiry has been stimulated, it seems, less by the posing of a direct question about the emergence of Israelite literature, than by an attempt to account for the pervasive presence in the Old Testament of a distinctive intellectual attitude (with its associated literary idiom) – at once rational and religious, down-to-earth and morally sensitive – of which 'Wisdom' is the most obtrusive concept. As long as this outlook was thought to be confined to the Jewish literature which enlarged explicitly on the concept of 'Wisdom' (Proverbs, Job, Ecclesiastes, Ecclesiasticus and the Wisdom of Solomon), it was possible to regard the phenomenon as a late (post-exilic) development in Israel, emanating from reflective (if somewhat elusive) 'sages', who, happily liberalized by wide international contacts, came near to qualifying as philosophers and gentlemen.

The rediscovery, however, during the last century, of the culture of ancient Egypt has established the existence of a mature 'classical' tradition at least two thousand years before the Greeks began to dominate the scene and there are now hopeful indications that Old Testament 'Wisdom' is at last being rescued from the students of Plato and interpreted in the less abstract and more relevant context of Egyptian scribal education. In the last twenty years, a silent revolution has been taking place in the learned journals. Connections with the 'Wisdom' tradition of Egypt have been detected in parts of the Old Testament far removed in date and *genre* from the book of Job – in the historical books, the liturgical poems of the Psalter, the oracles of the prophets and even in the law codes (not to mention such miscellaneous works as Daniel, Esther and Tobit).[1] Although the habit is hard to break, the continued use of 'Wisdom' as an umbrella term for so heterogeneous a collection of literary types, propounding, as they do, so many different kinds of theology, no longer makes much sense.[2] What justifies associating this ever-growing range of Old Testament material in a common tradition is neither a similar theological purpose nor a fixed literary *genre*, but, rather, an identifiable intellectual stance and literary idiom, which stem from a common educational background.

The 'Wisdom' tradition of the Old Testament is no more and no less than the 'classical' tradition of its educated men. This 'classical' tradition absorbed, of course, many new elements – Mesopotamian, Persian, Greek – during the course of its development over a thousand years, but it seems never to have departed fundamentally from the ethos and outlook of the scribal education which Solomon's new men introduced from Egypt into the emergent state of Israel. It is significant, not so much as one of the distinctive traditions in Israel's thinking, but as a major source of the categories and language in which Israel did *all* her thinking and gave articulation to her own distinctive convictions. To appreciate the medium is, as always, better to understand the message.

Since the Egyptian educational tradition was only the milieu of Israel's scribes and not their master, it is reflected in the books of the Old Testament with differing degrees of clarity. It is, for example, unambiguous in didactic writings like the book of Proverbs and elusive in the vehement and highly personal oracles of the prophets.[3] In the narrative literature of Solomon's age, when Israel's scribes were most directly and powerfully influenced by their Egyptian heritage, an undoubted affiliation may be detected. In reviewing narratives like the Joseph Story, the Succession Story, and the Yahwist's history of Israel, it is important to recognize that the case for tracing their origin to graduates of Israel's new scribal schools does not depend on establishing the adoption of any known Egyptian writing as a literary model and even less on proving that some incident or expression has been borrowed from a particular Egyptian source. All that we may reasonably expect to discover is that the *motifs* and style of these works sufficiently reflect what we know of the literature of the Egyptian schools to suggest a continuity of educational tradition.

THE JOSEPH STORY

In separating the Joseph Story from the less polished and more fragmentary sagas of the other patriarchs in the book of Genesis, scholars have at last caught up with their children.[4] This miniature novel displays a depth of psychological insight, a sense of situation and a command of language which have transformed a local-boy-makes-good story into an acknowledged literary masterpiece. It is remarkable that its main structure has survived at least two major 'refits' designed to serve the purposes of later editors. These amplifications are easier to detect in general than to identify with precision, but it is usually agreed that the episode of Judah and Tamar, the antiquarian list of Jacob's seventy descendants, the blessings of Jacob, and the miscellaneous collection of aphorisms on the twelve tribes should be disregarded as later intrusions.[5] It is also usually agreed that there is a double tradition in the main story itself. In one version, the father is called Israel and the 'good' brother Judah, whereas in the second version the father is called Jacob and the 'good' brother Reuben. Although there is no generally accepted view of the relationship between these two traditions, most scholars regard the 'Israel–Judah' version as the work of a scribe at Solomon's court.[6] It is arguable that the 'Jacob–Reuben' version, which includes the dream theme,[7] was spliced into the original story in the sixth century BC or later, to give encouragement to those Jews who were then dispersed abroad.[8]

The original story recounts how Joseph, the apple of his father's eye, was sold by his elder brothers into slavery and carried off to Egypt. After virtuously resisting the advances of his master's wife, Joseph enters the services of the Pharaoh himself and wins acclaim by organizing an ingenious scheme for creating a state monopoly of corn, which, in time of famine, enables his royal master to absorb the whole of the country's resources into state-ownership. As a reward, he is promoted to the office of Steward[9] and given as wife the daughter of a notable high priest. The day arrives when his wicked brothers are thrown on his mercy. Driven by famine, they come down to Egypt to buy corn and, without knowing it, receive their supplies from Joseph, who makes it a condition that they bring to him Benjamin, his favourite young brother. Israel, the old father, heartbroken at the prospect of losing yet another son, reluctantly agrees to Benjamin's being taken to Egypt. Joseph treats his brothers royally, discloses his identity, and sends them off rejoicing to collect their father and bring him also to Egypt for a great family reunion. On this occasion, they are received by the Pharaoh himself and given permission to settle in Goshen. When, eventually, the old father dies, Joseph and a great company from the Egyptian court take his body home for burial. Joseph lives to the ripe old age of 110 and he, too, is taken home for burial.

The success of young men exiled in foreign courts was a favourite theme of Egyptian story-writers. The *Story of Sinuhe*,[10] which has been described as the 'Robinson Crusoe' of Egyptian schoolboys and was constantly copied as a writing exercise from *c.* 1800–1000 BC, presents the Joseph Story in reverse. It recounts the adventures of an official of Pharaoh's court exiled in Syria, where, he reports, the ruler 'set me at the head of his children. He married me to his eldest daughter. He let me choose for myself of his country.... He made me ruler of a tribe of the choicest of his country.' Sinuhe accumulated great wealth and became the ruler's political adviser and commander of his army. In his old age, he returned to Egypt and received both promotion at court and the gratifying promise of a lavish burial. Another exile's success story, the *Tale of the Two Brothers*,[11] is preserved in a magnificent manuscript (now in the British Museum) which was copied by a pupil for the Scribe of Pharaoh's Treasury about 1225 BC. The fact that the two brothers are named after gods – Anubis and Bata – suggests that the tale had its origin in myth, but it has now been toned down and given a setting in the more nearly human world of fairy story. It begins, however, in an ordinary Egyptian village, where Bata, an eligible young bachelor, is working on his married brother's farm. One day, when he goes back to the house for more seed, he finds himself alone with his sister-in-law, who promptly tries to seduce him. The virtuous young man 'became enraged like a leopard' at the very suggestion of such impropriety and prudently rushed off. The wife then fakes evidence to suggest that Bata had beaten her up and concocts for the benefit of her husband a story of his attempted rape. In his rage, the husband plots to kill Bata, but God enables him to convince his brother of his integrity and innocence. The elder brother then returns home, kills his wife and sits 'in mourning for his younger brother'. Meanwhile, Bata has become a voluntary exile in Lebanon where the gods out of compassion give him a beautiful wife. She, however, has bigger game to hunt and makes her way to the Egyptian court, where she becomes the Great Lady of the Pharaoh. Here, she exploits her charms to have Bata killed, but his elder brother foils her evil designs, employs magical arts to bring Bata back to life, is introduced by him to the Pharaoh, and is then sent home laden with treasure. Bata's wife renews her plot to do away with him, but (with supernatural help) he survives, and, in the end, actually becomes Pharaoh and his elder brother the Crown Prince.

It would be going far beyond the evidence to suggest that either of these tales is the source of the Joseph Story, but equally it would be ignoring the obvious not to recognize that all three belong to a common literary tradition. In particular, it is generally acknowledged that Joseph's rejection of Potiphar's wife is strikingly similar to Bata's encounter with his sister-in-law.[12] The probability of a connection between them is not weakened, as is sometimes suggested,[13] by the fact that Bata rejects his sister-in-law's advances by appealing to social convention, instead of declaring outright that adultery is a 'sin against God'. In fact, Joseph's argument takes the same dutiful line: 'Think of my master. He does not know as much as I do about his own house, and he has entrusted me with all he has. He has given me authority in this house second only to his own, and has withheld nothing from me except you, because you are his wife. How can I do anything so wicked, and sin against God?.'[14] Even the recognition of adultery as a 'sin against God' is common ground between the two stories, as, indeed, it was between Egyptian and Hebrew morality as a whole.[15] It is reported that Bata 'prayed to the Re-Har-akhti, saying: "O my good lord, thou art he who judges the wicked from the just"'. It was the same god who protected Bata throughout his adventures, just as 'the Lord was with Joseph and kept faith with him, so that he won the favour of the governor of the Round Tower . . . and gave him success in everything.'[16]

It is remarkable that the biblical writer is content to allow the action of his story to take its own course, determined by the characters themselves, and to present God simply as saving them from the evil consequences of their decisions without in any way compromising their freedom. So far from being an interfering *deus ex machina*, he acts only as a discreet overruling Providence – 'that divinity that shapes our ends rough-hew them how we will': 'I am your brother Joseph whom you sold into Egypt. Now do not be distressed or take it amiss that you sold me into slavery here; it was God who sent me ahead of you to save men's lives. . . . So it was not you who sent me here, but God. . . . You meant to do me harm; but God meant to bring good out of it.'[17] This concept of a cooperative relationship between human freedom and divine control is a commonplace in the school-texts of the Egyptian scribes[18] and the significance it allows to the actions of men is everywhere presupposed in the distinctive style of their short stories. It has been noticed, for example, that in the *Story of Sinuhe* the character of the hero 'is revealed through his clearly established attitudes and re-actions to the various situations in which he finds himself',[19] and another Egyptologist has made a similar observation about the *Tale of the Two Brothers*:

It is . . . of some interest that at no point does the story-teller comment on the conduct of his characters, or express an opinion about even the most unsympathetic of them. In Egypt the tone of stories is always objective – it is the rule – and only the behaviour of the protagonists and their remarks make it possible to distinguish the good from the bad.[20]

The autonomy of the characters in the Joseph Story and the theological reticence of its writer are congruous with the view that he was heir to the distinctive tradition of the Egyptian scribes.

This tradition took it for granted that (under Providence) the scribes ruled the roost. Only in Egypt is it conceivable that a time-serving and ambitious bureaucrat like Sinuhe should have become a schoolboy's hero. Similar strange criteria are presupposed by the biblical writer's intention that Joseph should win the reader's unqualified admiration. He is introduced at the age of seventeen as bringing his father 'a bad report' on his brother's management of the flock.[21] At the age of thirty, he advises the Pharaoh to appoint con-trollers over the land to cope with the food situation and is immediately promoted to the office of Steward. After his investiture, he proceeds on 'a tour of inspection throughout the country',[22] displaying that 'zeal, firmness and efficiency', which is so often enjoined and claimed in late-Egyptian scribal correspondence.[23] Joseph's manipulation of his brothers may show mastery of man-management, but it is hardly justified by his affection for Benjamin.[24] He is the very embodiment of the two-fold wisdom commended in Proverbs: 'Forethought and diligence are sure of profit.'[25]

It is again the book of Proverbs which suggests an explanation of one of Joseph's most striking individual characteristics – his refusal to reveal his feelings in public: 'Joseph was overcome; his feelings for his brother mastered him, and he was near to tears. So he went into the inner room and wept. Then he washed his face and came out; and, holding back his feelings, he ordered the meal to be served.'[26] Such public reserve, which is so effectively abandoned in the private recognition scenes,[27] is the sang-froid demanded of the civil servant, both in the book of Proverbs and the scribal literature of Egypt.[28] The eulogy of a scribal teacher at the end of the Papyrus Lansing is particularly illuminating on this and other points:

You are at home in all manner of ways, like Sight and Hearing. You are a good helper of your dependants; your large meals are copious like a high inundation. You are one that abounds in food and knows how to direct it unto all men whom you will, like a surging sea. *You are a magistrate in calmness*, a son of praised ones; one beloved of all men who is under the favour of the king. . . . *You are one reticent in counsel*, one who weighs his answer; your abomination is obscene talk since your birth. . . . You are one select of speeches and versed in saying them; all that you have said has been accurate.[29]

That the author of the Joseph Story avoided turning his hero into a dummy civil servant spouting proverbial wisdom bears eloquent testimony to the mature tradition out of which he wrote. Language was the basic tool of the scribe's profession, as the eulogy noted, and it was cultivated with meticulous craftsmanship – to produce, for example, the superbly limpid and moving speech of Judah, which precipitates Joseph's final recognition of his brothers:

Our father, my lord, then said to us, 'You know that my wife bore me two sons. One left me, and I said, "He must have been torn to pieces." I have not seen him to this day. If you take this one from me as well, and he comes to any harm, then you will bring down my grey hairs in trouble to the grave.' Now, my lord, when I return to my father without the boy – and remember, his life is bound up with the boy's – what will happen is this: he will see that the boy is not with us and will die, and your servants will have brought down our father's grey hairs in sorrow to the grave. Indeed, my lord, it was I who went surety for the boy to my father. I said, 'If I do not bring him back to you, then you shall hold me guilty all my life.' Now, my lord, let me remain in place of the boy as your lordship's slave, and let him go with his brothers. How can I return to my father without the boy? I could not bear to see the misery which my father would suffer.[30]

The confident and skilled use of dialogue in this passage is a feature of the story as a whole.

It is the literary style of Solomon's scribes which provides the best evidence for their familiarity with things Egyptian, but scholars have usually given more attention (and especially in studying the Joseph Story) to the possible Egyptian colouring of such features of the biblical narrative as names, titles and vocabulary, together with any details thought to reflect specific social and political institutions. The conclusion which seems to emerge after generations of intense scrutiny and research is that precise connections of the Joseph Story with any particular historical situation in Egypt cannot be confidently established, but that Egyptian influence is to be found in a generalized and, sometimes, romanticized form.[31]

Even if it is clear that the Joseph Story was written by a Jerusalem scribe educated in the classical literary tradition of Egypt, his purpose in undertaking the work still remains obscure. Later editors have exploited the narrative to expound the tribal structure of Israel and to illustrate the tradition that 'Jacob and his sons went down to Egypt', but such reinterpretation provides no clue to the original writer's intention. The most suggestive hint is to be found in the Egyptian practice of writing stories as political propaganda. The *Story of Sinuhe* has recently been interpreted as an unofficial political novel, written to support the Twelfth Dynasty after the conspiracy against its first king, Ammenemes I, and to encourage, among other policies, its new *entente cordiale* with Syria.[32] Despite the obvious differences in presentation, it is probable that a comparable political and diplomatic purpose underlies the Story of Joseph.

With this in mind, the political implications of the names of his principal characters assume an importance too often overlooked; the choice of Joseph, Israel and Judah can hardly have been casual or gone unobserved. It was only in the reigns of David and Solomon that the tribe of Judah came into prominence, and it was the union of the northern and southern tribal groups under these two kings which gave currency to 'the house of Joseph' and 'the house of Judah' as parallel terms. It is also probable that the adoption of 'Israel' as the name of the ancestor of the twelve tribes presupposes the 'family reunion' achieved by David: 'David ruled over *the whole of Israel* and maintained law and justice among all his people.'[33]

In the light of the political overtones of these names, it is reasonable to speculate that the Joseph Story represents the attempt of a court scribe to illustrate the claim made in the Annals of Solomon that 'all through his reign Judah and Israel continued at peace . . . from Dan to Beersheba'. His flattering portrait of Joseph as the supremely successful statesman, who established the Pharaoh's absolute control of his kingdom, may well reflect his admiration for Solomon's régime; it may also represent his awareness that its very existence depended on the continuing goodwill of the 'house of Joseph', whose power in the north was as great as it was potentially dangerous.[34]

THE SUCCESSION STORY

The stylistic features which distinguish the Joseph Story from the saga material in Genesis also set the Succession Story apart from its context in the second book of Samuel.[35] As the widely-accepted title for these fourteen chapters suggests, most scholars recognize them as comprising an originally independent composition written in the early years of Solomon's reign to defend, in the face of opposition, his succession to the throne: 'Thus Solomon's royal power was securely established.'[36] In this respect, it resembles the Egyptian *Instruction of Ammenemes I*, composed *c*. 1960 BC by the author of the *Satire of the Trades*, to justify the reign of the king and the claim of his son, Sesostris I (1971–1928 BC), to succeed him on the throne.[37] Although this work was still part of the syllabus in the scribal schools of the Ramesside period and, therefore, conceivably known to the scribes of Solomon's court, its extreme brevity and austere auto-biographical style rule out the possibility of its having directly inspired the author of the Succession Story. Nevertheless, he may well have been influenced by the long-established tradition of royalist propaganda it represents, of which the *Prophecy of Neferty* (*c*. 1990 BC)[38] and the *Story of Sinuhe* (*c*. 1960 BC)[39] were further popular examples.

It is, however, the Succession Story's approximation to the modern novel which suggests (at first blush, paradoxically) that it was written under the influence of the Egyptian educational tradition. The rise of the English novel with Defoe, Richardson and Fielding in the eighteenth century was made possible, it has been suggested, by the emergence of philosophical realism in the seventeenth century.[40] This revolutionary rejection of the Greek tradition in western culture, with its emphasis on the divine, the timeless and the universal, in favour of the experiences and autonomous decisions of particular men at particular times and in particular places, cleared the ground for the stylistic 'realism' of the new *genre*. However, much of what was fought for in the seventeenth and eighteenth centuries AD was simply taken for granted in the ancient culture of Egypt before the fateful emergence of Plato and Greek metaphysics.

The Egyptian scribal tradition was emphatically empirical. Education was primarily designed to equip officials to cope expertly with particular practical problems and it is no accident that the kind of mathematics taught in the schools shows a complete ignorance of theoretical principles and could have served only the immediate needs of everyday life.[41] Even the literature of the scribes is dominated by everyday life. It is probably the same empirical outlook which accounts for the fact that Egyptian writers never rose to the majestic heights of the epic form, and when they adopted mythological material they invariably brought it down to the level of earth-bound story-telling – the literary form in which they conspicuously excelled. Literature in Egypt was not, as so often in antiquity, the handmaid of religion.[42]

This emphasis, which has been described – intelligibly if not very accurately – as 'secular humanism', points to the common ground between the pre-metaphysical tradition of Egypt and the post-metaphysical tradition of Europe and illuminates the emergence in both of the 'realism' characteristic of the novelist. As a recent writer has suggested,

> It is therefore likely that a measure of secularization was an indispensable condition for the rise of the new genre. . . . The novel, Georg Lukács has written, is the epic of a world forsaken by God; it presents, in de Sade's phrase, 'le tableau des mœurs séculaires'. . . . We can say that the novel requires a world view which is centred on the social relationships between individual persons; and this involves secularization as well as individualism, because until the end of the seventeenth century the individual was not conceived as wholly autonomous, but as an element in a picture which depended on divine persons for its meaning.[43]

The Succession Story is entirely made up of 'the social relationships between individual persons'. Although the basic plot is structured by the systematic elimination of Solomon's rivals for the throne – Amnon, Absalom and Adonijah –

their fate is not determined *ab extra*, but by their free individual response in an intricate complex of entirely credible human situations. Amnon loses his life through raping Absalom's sister. Absalom's fratricide leads to exile, which, aided by David's chronic indecisiveness, engenders a rebellion, ultimately crushed by Absalom's death at the hands of Joab, his former ally. Adonijah wins the support of Joab in his bid for the throne, but is outwitted by a court conspiracy using Bathsheba as its tool and finally seals his fate by employing the same intermediary (David's faded first-love) in an attempt to obtain the beautiful Abishag, brought in to comfort the king in his impotent old age.

The action covers some twenty years and, as Erich Auerbach has pointed out, the author shows an awareness of time which is not to be found in most writers of antiquity:

Achilles and Odysseus are splendidly described in many well-ordered words, epithets cling to them, their emotions are constantly displayed in their words and deeds – but they have no development, and their life-histories are clearly set forth once and for all. . . . But what a road, what a fate, lie . . . between David the harp player, persecuted by his lord's jealousy, and the old king, surrounded by violent intrigues, whom Abishag the Shunammite warmed in his bed, and he knew her not![44]

David, depicted with that open recognition of his human frailty which (rather surprisingly) characterizes the realistic portrayal of the Pharaoh both in literature and art,[45] is the central figure of a drama teeming with subordinate characters skillfully woven into the fabric of the plot. The writer's psychological interest extends even to men of action like Absalom and Joab, who are brought alive with the authentic ambiguity of human persons by being presented in revealing situations rather than pickled in descriptive prose. This fascination with people is further confirmed by the writer's prodigality with his minor characters – the knowing Jonadab, the chaste Tamar in her long, sleeved robe, the wise and voluble woman of Tekoah, the eager young Ahimaaz with his particular way of running, Saul's grandson Mephi-bosheth, crippled in both feet, the endearing octogenarian, Barzillai, with his son Kimham, the fanatical Shimei pelting David with stones, and the old biddy of Abel, who saved her city by procuring Sheba's head.[46]

The reappearance of these minor characters after their first introduction contributes unobtrusively to the unity of the work, as does the subtle repetition of such *motifs* as that of the ten concubines.[47] They are also ingeniously used to vary the pace of the narrative and to create suspense. David's exchange with Ittai the Gittite seems interminable after his dramatic flight from Jerusalem;[48] Ziba's two asses' load of food is laboriously investigated as the reader waits impatiently for news of his master's allegiance;[49] Ahimaaz and Jonathan, carrying a warning vital to David's welfare, are forced to hide in somebody's courtyard – a splendidly exciting episode sandwiched between urgent commands: 'Now send quickly to David. . . . Over the water at once, make haste!';[50] later, it is again Ahimaaz who lowers the pace and heightens the tension between Absalom's death and David's receiving the news.[51] This last incident is the supreme example of the writer's skill in the use of dramatic irony,[52] which, since for the reader the question of the succession has already been settled, is the context of the story as a whole.

Much of the superb artistry of this work is to be ascribed, not simply to a general intellectual milieu of the kind which encouraged literary realism, but to the specific preoccupations of the scribal schools. Nearly all the rapid changes of scene and, more important, the constant establishment of a contemporaneous relationship between different scenes as foreground and background, which, of course, permits dramatic irony and creates an awareness of dimension and depth, depend upon the unremitting activity of *messengers*.[53] It is probable that this dominant feature of the story is connected with the special emphasis on the training needed by a professional messenger in the curriculum of the scribal schools:

If thou art a man of intimacy, whom one great man sends to another, be thoroughly reliable when he sends thee. Carry out the errand for him as he has spoken. Do not be reserved about what is said to thee, and beware of any act of forgetfulness. Grasp hold of truth, and do not exceed it. Mere gratification is by no means to be repeated. Struggle against making words worse, thus making one great man hostile to another through vulgar speech.[54]

Ptahhotep's fastidious attitude to speech was even more apposite for the scribe who attained the exalted rank of counsellor:

If thou art a man of standing, one sitting in the counsels of his lord, summon thy resources for good. If thou art silent, it is better than *teftef*-plants. If thou speakest, thou shouldst know how thou canst explain difficulties. *It is a real craftsman who can speak in counsel, for speaking is more difficult than any labour.*[55]

It is precisely this difficult art which the writer of the Succession Story chooses to demonstrate in the formal court speeches of the rival counsellors, Ahithophel and Hushai (of whom the first, the reader is told, was driven to suicide by his wounded professional pride). Their stylized rhetoric came, no doubt, straight from the school manuals:

I will bring all the people over to you *as a bride is brought to her husband.* . . . You know that your father and the men with him are hardened warriors and *savage as a bear in the wilds robbed of her cubs.* . . . My advice is this. Wait until the whole of Israel, from Dan to Beersheba, is gathered about you, *countless as grains of sand on the sea-shore.* . . . Then we shall . . . descend on him *like dew falling on the ground.*[56]

The art of speaking, as both the Egyptian Instructions and the book of Proverbs testify, was to be cultivated in private conversation as well as in public council. It is almost certainly this civilized concern which explains the confident use of dialogue in Egyptian literature – in works like the *Tale of the Two Brothers* and the *Story of Sinuhe*, and even in reports of official missions, like the incomparable *Journey of Wenamun* (*c.* 1100 BC).[57] Wenamun, a temple official sent to Byblos to obtain timber for his god's ceremonial barge, discovered the prince of that city to be a hard man of business:

I found him sitting in his upper room, with his back turned to a window, so that the waves of the great Syrian sea broke against the back of his head. So I said to him: 'May Amon favour you!' But he said to me: 'How long, up to today, since you came from the place where Amon is?' So I said to him: 'Five months and one day up to now.' And he said to me: 'Well you're truthful. . . .' And he answered and said to me: 'On what business have you come?' So I told him: 'I have come after the woodwork for the great and august barque of Amon-Re, King of the Gods. Your father did it, your grandfather did it, and you will do it too!' So I spoke to him. But he said to me: 'To be sure, they did it! And if you give me something for doing it, I will do it! Why, when my people carried out this commission, Pharaoh – life, prosperity, health! – sent six ships loaded with Egyptian goods, and they unloaded them into their storehouses! You – what is it that you're bringing me – me also?' And he had the journal rolls of his fathers brought, and he had them read out in my presence, and they found a thousand *deben* of silver and all kinds of things in his scrolls.

The arresting dramatic quality of this encounter, with its effective contrast between the ingratiating courtesy of the envoy and the brusque efficiency of the prince, is frequently paralleled in the Succession Story. The Bathsheba–Uriah scene, for example, from the tranquil economy of its first sentence – 'One evening David got up from his couch and, as he walked about on the roof of the palace, he saw from there a woman bathing, and she was very beautiful' – gradually mounts, largely through dialogue, to an intolerable tension, as the reader awaits the king's reaction to the news of Uriah's death. Then, with consummate skill, it is given in flat platitudes – the *lingua franca* of the hypocrite: 'Give Joab this message: "Do not let this distress you – there is no knowing where the sword will strike; press home your attack on the city, and you will take it and raze it to the ground"; and tell him to take heart.' On any reckoning the Succession Story is the work of an educated man writing in a mature literary tradition.[58]

That this tradition was Egyptian is further indicated by the distinctive view it takes of the relationship between human freedom and divine control. As in the Joseph Story, the participants in the drama are left free to satisfy their own lusts and pursue their own ambitions, but in and through the consequences of their actions, God is represented as achieving his determined plan: 'It was the Lord's purpose to frustrate Ahithophel's good advice and so bring disaster upon Absalom.'[59] Apart from such rare references to the secret participation of God in this apparently closed circuit of sin-and-suffering, there broods only a dark fatalism: 'let him [God] do what he pleases with me . . . who can question it?'[60] Such resignation, quivering on the edge of Ecclesiastes' scepticism, is a marked feature of the later Ramesside Instructions,[61], but the concept of a God 'who hides himself', the Invisible who controls the visible, is as early in Egyptian thought as the *Instruction for Merikare* (c. 2100 BC): 'Generation passes generation among men, and the god, who knows men's characters, has hidden himself. But there is none who can withstand the Lord of the Hand: he is the one who attacks what the eyes can see.'[62] To represent this theology of the 'hidden God' as a sophisticated product of Solomon's 'Age of Enlightenment' is, probably, to exaggerate its intellectual stature and to associate it misleadingly with the attenuated and more thoroughly rationalized piety of the modern period.[63] There are, however, genuine and fascinating links between the Egyptian–Israelite cultural tradition and that of the modern West, since, for the representation of human affairs, it is a matter of indifference whether God operates secretly, or not at all. It is not surprising that the writer of the Succession Story has sometimes been accorded a place in the development of man's quest for self-understanding, which challenges that often claimed for the Greek historians some five hundred years later.

THE YAHWIST'S HISTORY

The noble design of the first history of Israel is now concealed from the casual observer by the 'improvements' and renovations of later contributors to the complex architecture of the Pentateuch. It is as though the single vision which, happily, still informs the Cathedral of Salisbury had been fragmented by the replacement of the spire by a Florentine campanile and the extension of the Choir in Victorian Gothic. The Yahwist (as convention demands the anonymous historian be called) did not enjoy, however, the advantage of the Sarum architect's virgin stone and Purbeck marble, but was compelled to build with a mass of old material – tribal sagas, sanctuary legends, liturgical recitals, aetiological myths, and so on – no longer raw or malleable enough to fit easily into his overall plan. His achievement in creating a single, unified and coherent structure is an eloquent testimony to the power of his intellect and the strength of his motivation.

The driving force behind the Yahwist's history is an enthusiastic awareness that he is a member of a society burgeoning with vitality and untold possibilities. Under David and Solomon, the loose confederation of Israel's tribes had been transformed into a united nation, had risen with startling rapidity to the prestige of an imperial power, and was now luxuriating in its new access to the commerce and culture of its old-established neighbours in the Ancient Near East. This is the extraordinary situation which the Yahwist seeks both to celebrate and explain. The need for an explanation, which is not immediately obvious, could have occurred only to a man who was as alive to what Israel had been as to what it had so recently become, and, more than that, as realistic about the forces which threaten civilized society as about the advantages which accrue from it. The Yahwist grounds both his celebration and his explanation of the new state of Israel in his people's basic conviction that they owed their very existence in history to the gracious initiative and protection of their God. With remarkable courage and intellectual stamina, he detaches this faith from its original tight connection with the

Exodus from Egypt and articulates its significance on a universal scale. Without sacrificing historical concreteness to this new rationalized perspective, he pulls together all the diverse traditions in the tribal background of his people along a single 'story-line', and presents Yahweh as disclosing through this particular history the controlling purpose of *all* history, since time first began. Thus, from the Yahwist's point of view, Solomon's new state is neither an upstart among the nations, nor a traitor to Israel's ancient traditions; on the contrary, it is the fulfilment in history of a promise made to Abraham, which, in its turn, was Yahweh's providential response to his creatures' manifest inability to order life on their own.

Beginning with the splendidly matter-of-fact statement, 'When the Lord God made earth and heaven . . .', the Yahwist's history is fairly evenly distributed through Genesis, the first half of Exodus and the middle chapters of Numbers, and now ends when, after its wanderings, a united Israel is poised on the brink of the Promised Land. It is at this point that Moses commissions his men to spy out Palestine and, in doing so, adopts an idiom which echoes school geography lessons as clearly as the questioning at the end of Hori's *Satirical Letter*:

Make your way up by the Negeb, and go on into the hill-country. See what the land is like, and whether the people who live there are strong or weak, few or many. See whether it is easy or difficult country in which they live, and whether the cities in which they live are weakly defended or well fortified; is the land fertile or barren, and does it grow trees or not?[64]

Whether or not the work once continued with an account of the conquest and settlement of Canaan (as some scholars suppose), there can be no doubt that possession of the land and the establishment of the monarchy represent the goal to which it points. Both are presupposed in the threefold promise given to Abraham, with which (after the first eleven 'universal' chapters) the history of Israel proper begins: 'The

147

The literature of the scribes

Lord said to Abram, "Leave your own country, your kins-
men, and your father's house, and go to a country that I will
show you. I will make you into a great nation, I will bless
you and make your name so great that it shall be used in
blessings".'[65] It has recently been argued that the Abrahamic
traditions were of especial interest to the Jerusalem court[66]
and a further connection between the Yahwist's allegiance to
the monarchy and his handling of traditional material has
been found in the presentation of Moses as a king.[67] His
loyalty is certainly fully explicit in the 'prediction', attri-
buted to Balaam, of the 'star' of David, rising to lead his
people in imperial conquest.[68]

Although it is academically fashionable to assert that Egypt
had no historians and was incapable of making any contribution to the beginnings of historical writing in Israel,[69] it may
be thought that this *genre* is altogether too complex for so
dogmatic a view. Despite all the gaps and ambiguities, it has,
nevertheless, proved possible for modern scholars to piece
together the fortuitous remains of Egypt and write a connected account of the nation under the Pharaohs. Records
from tombs and temples provide lists and annalistic material
in plenty and these are often given a historical context by
narratives in both literary and pictorial form. If facts and a
motive for recording them are among the ingredients of
historical writing, it may be said that the civilization of the
Nile had undoubtedly made a start.

The Egyptians, as we have seen, were particularly devoted
to the writing of stories and it is relevant to recall that these
lively narratives invariably present the actions and motives of
their characters with penetrating insight and remarkable
objectivity. Autobiography and prophecy were often used
for political purposes and official reports sometimes dressed
up as works of fiction; as the *genres* multiplied and over-
lapped, the Egyptian scribes came at least within striking
distance of 'genuine' history. Even schoolboys were copying
historical inscriptions as early as the sixteenth century B C.
One such writing exercise, the so-called Carnarvon Tablet,

Fig. 24   Relief from Karnak depicting the attack of Sethos I on Qadesh (Dynasty XIX). W. Stevenson Smith comments: 'Something more specific was now attempted in the way of historical record, and a sense of dramatic conflict was achieved in a more topical narrative style than had hitherto been contemplated by an Egyptian artist. . . . The landscape is economically reduced to a few trees and bushes set along irregularly curving lines beneath the crenellated walls of the fortress manned by an agitated garrison. The pressing immediacy of the attack is further heightened by the little figure of a herdsman driving his cattle off to the right.' (*Art and Architecture of Ancient Egypt.*)

which gives a vivid account of the campaign of Kamose against the Hyksos and was at one time dismissed as a mere 'literary' text, has now been authenticated by two stelae discovered at Karnak.[70] It would be equally imprudent to deny historical status to the eye-witness accounts of the final campaigns against the Hyksos, which are contained in the laconic autobiography of Ahmose, a soldier who himself fought with the troops of Amosis (1570–1546 BC) and Tuthmosis I (1525–1512 BC).[71]

If the connecting as well as the collecting of facts and events is a *sine qua non* of the historian's task, it would not be too bold to claim that a new approach to it was made in Egypt during the Nineteenth Dynasty (1320–1200 BC). The principal evidence comes from the 'war-pictures' of the temples. It has

Fig. 25 Relief from the Ramesseum – the funerary temple of Ramesses II on the west bank at Thebes (Dynasty XIX). Ramesses II is seen charging the Hittite forces before the fortified city of Qadesh. The Pharaoh's chariot is fitted with a quiver for javelins as well as one for arrows (a development since the 14th century BC) and its wheels have six spokes. The representation of the other chariots as having wheels with eight spokes instead of six is an error of the modern copyist.

been pointed out that a military victory is 'no longer shown only ideographically as simply the king smiting a vanquished foe, but also is expanded into a series of elaborate scenes providing a narrative.'[72] This development in 'visual historiography' may be observed in the commemoration of the Syrian campaigns of Sethos I (1318–1304 BC) and, supremely, in the portrayal of the Battle of Qadesh, which with typical self-assertiveness was commissioned by Ramesses II. This has been called 'a unique attempt to place the different parts of a complicated narrative in factual relationship to one another'[73] and it would be difficult to find a better description of the Yahwist's achievement as a historian.

It is, however, the literary record of the Battle of Qadesh which sheds most light on the historiography of the Yahwist. Both the Egyptian and the biblical writer present their story of conquest as a 'Holy War' and it is the ascription of the action to the Divine Warrior which gives unity to the narrative, as well as a powerful motivation to the writer. The Egyptian inscription was written, no doubt, for the greater glory of the Pharaoh, but formally it is presented as a celebration of the mighty acts of Amun, his god. It consists largely of speeches by Ramesses at a point in the battle when he found himself surrounded by Hittite enemy forces and deserted by his own troops:

And his majesty said: 'What is it then, my father Amun? Hath a father indeed forgotten his son? Have I done aught without thee? Have I not gone or stood still because of thine utterance? And I never swerved from the counsels of thy mouth. How great is the great lord of Thebes, too great to suffer the foreign peoples to come nigh him! What are these Asiatics to thee, Amun? Wretches that know not God!..' Amun hearkeneth unto me and cometh, when I cry to him. He stretcheth out his hand to me, and I rejoice; he calleth out behind me: 'Forward, forward! I am with thee, I thy father. Mine hand is with thee, and I am of more avail than an hundred thousand men, I, the lord of victory, that loveth strength.' I have found my courage again . . . I find that the two thousand five hundred chariots, in whose midst I was, lie hewn in pieces before my steeds. Not one of them hath found his hand to fight. Their hearts are become faint in their bodies for fear, their arms are all become powerless. They are unable to shoot, and have not the heart to take their lances. . . . I shouted out to my army: 'Steady, steady your hearts, my soldiers. Ye behold my victory, I being alone. But Amun is my protector, and his hand is with me.' . . . The foreign countries who see me shall speak of my name as far as the farthest lands which are unknown. . . . Now when my foot-soldiers and chariotry saw that . . . Amun, my father, was joined with me and made every land straw before me, they approached one by one . . . and they found that all peoples, among whom I had forced my way, were lying slaughtered in heaps. [74]

In the Yahwist's history, we find remarkably similar features – the complaint that God has forgotten his chosen, his sovereignty over the godless nations, his superiority to the military might of mere men, his ability to strike the enemy with panic and render them powerless, and his final act of total slaughter. The writer first uses this 'Holy War' theme as a unifying thread for the diverse patriarchal material in Genesis:

I am the Lord, the God of your father Abraham and the God of Isaac. This land on which you are lying I will give to you and your descendants. They shall be countless as the dust upon the earth, and you shall spread far and wide, to north and south, to east and west. All the families of the earth shall pray to be blessed as you and your descendants are blessed. I will be with you, and I will protect you wherever you go and will bring you back to this land; for I will not leave you until I have done all that I have promised.[75]

It is, however, with the story of the Exodus, presented in a way which is sometimes reminiscent of the accounts of the expulsion of the Hyksos from Egypt,[76] that the historian has the best opportunity of exploiting his concept of Yahweh as the Divine Warrior. After his account of the plagues, for which he is indebted to Egyptian folklore,[77] the Yahwist records the first 'murmuring in the wilderness':

Pharaoh was almost upon them when the Israelites looked up and saw the Egyptians close behind. In their terror *they clamoured to the Lord for help* and said to Moses, 'Were there no graves in Egypt, that you should have brought us here to die in the wilderness? See what you have done to us by bringing us out of Egypt! . . . We would rather be slaves to the Egyptians than die here in the wilderness.' '*Have no fear*,' Moses answered; 'stand firm and see the deliverance that the Lord will bring you this day; for as sure as you see the Egyptians now, you will never see them again. *The Lord will fight for you; you have only to be still.*' . . . In the morning watch the

38 Painting from the Theban tomb of a 'Scribe keeping account of the corn of Amun', that is, a temple official (Dynasty XVIII). The well-stocked garden has date-palms, mandrakes, sycamores and vines. The pool abounds in fish, water-fowl, papyrus plants and poppies.

39 Painting from the Theban tomb of a high-priest under Tuthmosis III (Dynasty XVIII). From left to right, a prince of Crete kisses the ground, a Hittite prince kneels with upraised hands, a prince of Tunep offers his infant son and, finally, a prince of Crete presents a Minoan bull's head.

40   The first of a series of six reliefs on the Libyan war from the temple of Ramesses III at Medinet Habu (Dynasty XX). Ramesses III (seated) receives the sickle-sword from the god Amun. This divine sanctioning of the war is witnessed by the ibis-headed god Thoth (on the left) and the moon-god Khons (on the right).

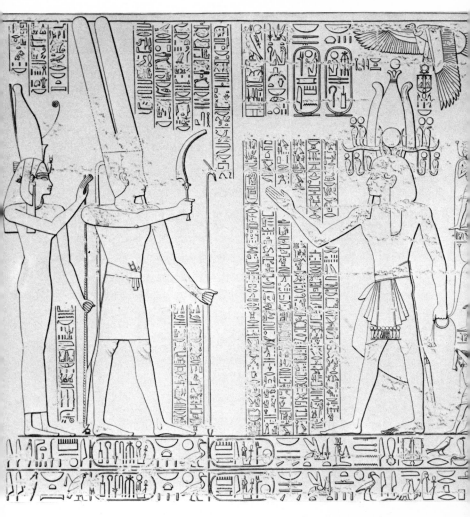

41 Relief from the temple of Ramesses III at Medinet Habu (Dynasty XX). Ramesses III leads three files of captives from the Sea Peoples to the god Amun and his wife Mut. In the inscription before the king, he praises Amun: 'Thy strong arm is that which is before me, over-throwing their seed. How great is thy strength, O Lord of the Gods! For he who relies upon that which thou hast ordained possesses king-ship, while everyone who walks upon thy way possesses peace.'

42 Limestone stela (height 44 cm.) from Amarna (Dynasty XVIII).
Akhenaten and Nefertiti are portrayed with their three eldest daughters,
as they receive the breath of life from the sun-disc Aten. Akhenaten is
giving an earring to one of his daughters, while his wife fondles the
other two on her knee.

43 Gold diadem from the royal tombs of Byblos (19th–18th century
BC). The hooded cobra in the centre is an Egyptian royal symbol; the
decoration of the diadem is of Egyptian signs of well-being and life.

Lord looked down on the Egyptian army through the pillar of fire and cloud, and *he threw them into a panic. . . .* That day the Lord saved Israel from the power of Egypt, and *the Israelites saw the Egyptians lying dead on the sea-shore.* When Israel saw the great power which the Lord had put forth against Egypt, all the people feared the Lord, and *they put their faith in him* and in Moses his servant.[78]

This lamentable concept of 'Holy War' and the quietist faith which was its counterpart survived long and was profoundly influential in Hebrew thought, but it began as part of the royal theology of Solomon's scribes, whose knowledge of the Pharaonic tradition contributed significantly to the Yahwist's achievement as the first historian of Israel.[79]

The Yahwist's dominant theological concern might well have sapped the vitality of the characters in his story and reduced them, as happened later in the books of Chronicles, to a succession of plaster saints. That such a disaster was avoided is obvious at a glance and so is the reason: the author is heir to that lively narrative tradition which underlies all the scribal literature of Solomon's court.[80] For example, in the Yahwist's masterly rewriting of the old legend which legitimatized the cult of Mamre, not only is the detail of the setting observed with splendid precision (as in the story of the rape of Tamar), but its three characters – the rash Sarah, the silent Abraham, and the penetrating Visitor – are vividly sketched with the utmost economy. The discussion between the Lord and Abraham about the fate of Sodom and Gomorrah – 'I must go down and see whether their deeds warrant the outcry which has reached me. I am resolved to know the truth' – could have taken place in Jerusalem any day of the week between the king and one of his counsellors, or, indeed, such a petitioner as the wise woman of Tekoah.[81] Again, the two stories which begin, 'By this time Abraham had become a very old man', and 'King David was now a very old man', have more in common than the problem of the succession.[82] They both reveal the literary craftsmanship of the Jerusalem scribes, their belief in the secret working of Providence and

their professional interest in successful diplomacy. The story
of Rebecca, in particular, reflects the ethos of the Egyptian
scribal schools, as illustrated, for example, by the *Instruction
of Ani*:

Take to thyself a wife while thou art still a youth, that she may
produce a son for thee. . . . Teach him to be a man.[83] . . . Be on thy
guard against a woman from abroad. . . . Do not talk a lot. Be
silent, and thou wilt be happy. . . . Pray thou with a loving heart,
all the words of which are hidden, and he will do what thou
needest. . . . Go every day according to the prescribed way, that
thou mayest walk with regard to precedence. . . . When thou art a
young man and takest to thyself a wife and art settled in thy house,
set thy eye on how thy mother gave birth to thee and all her
bringing thee up as well.[84]

The Yahwist handles his story with comparable presuppositions:

You will not take a wife for my son from the women of the
Canaanites in whose land I dwell; you must go to my own country
and to my own kindred to find a wife for my son Isaac. . . . Before
he had finished praying silently, he saw Rebecca coming out with
her water-jug on her shoulder. . . . The girl was very beautiful. . . .
The man was watching quietly to see whether or not the Lord had
made his journey successful. . . . I have been guided by the Lord. . . .
I will not eat until I have delivered my message. . . . I am the servant
of Abraham. The Lord has greatly blessed my master, and he has
become a man of power. . . . This is from the Lord; we can say
nothing for or against. . . . She shall be the wife of your master's
son, as the Lord has decreed. . . . So she became his wife, and he
loved her and was consoled for the death of his mother.[85]

It is precisely this 'human' interest and psychological insight
('It is not good for the man to be alone. I will provide a
partner for him') which distinguish the Yahwist's story of
Man's Creation and Fall[86] from the priestly cosmology of the
first chapter of Genesis and its background in Babylonian
and Canaanite mythology.[87] What might in different hands
have been an overwhelming manifestation of *mysterium
tremendum* is brought within the essentially domestic 'homes-

Fig. 26 Relief from the temple of Luxor (Dynasty XVIII). The ram-headed god Khnum (on the right) creates the prince Amenophis III and his *ka*, his *alter ego*, on a potter's wheel. The goddess Hathor (on the left) holds out the *ankh* sign, the emblem of life.

and-gardens' range of the scribe and is presented in typical short-story style: 'The man and his wife heard the sound of the Lord God walking in the garden in the cool of the day and hid from the Lord God among the trees of the garden.' Is not this a private garden, such as Egyptian boys in their writing exercises promised to their masters and the temple-scribe Ani hoped his son would one day be able to afford?[88] When, as is generally agreed, the section on the four-fold river of Eden is discounted as a later amplification,[89] again and again it is the tradition of Egypt rather than that of Mesopotamia which illuminates the distinctive features of the narrative.

The 'mist' which 'used to rise out of the earth and water all the surface of the ground' is better interpreted (with the New English Bible) as a 'flood', and then it begins to look un-commonly like the Egyptians' familiar experience of the Nile.[90] The creation of the first man 'from the dust of the ground' uses the Egyptian symbol of the potter's wheel, which is depicted, for example, in a bas-relief at Luxor com-memorating the birth of Amenophis III.[91] This scene also shows the child receiving 'the breath of life', a common concept throughout Egyptian art and literature, including the famous *Hymn to Aten*, much of which is echoed in Psalm 104.[92] Before the first man is provided with a suitable partner, he is given the animals for company and, if the writer were familiar with the *onomastica* of the scribal schools, it is natural that he should record that 'the man gave names to all cattle, to the birds of heaven, and to every wild animal'.[93] The description of the creation of the first woman is as down-to-earth as that of the first man and smacks more of surgical reality than sacred mystery: 'And so the Lord God *put the man into a trance*, and while he slept, he took one of his ribs and *closed the flesh over the place*. The Lord God then *built up the rib* . . . into a woman.'[94] It is wholly characteristic of the writer's tradition that marriage should be represented as the goal of creation. The Israelite scribes followed their Egyptian models in exalting family life, although they were probably ignorant of the fact that no less a person than the Pharaoh Akhenaten had had himself portrayed with Queen Nefertiti nursing their children and Tutankhamun, their son-in-law, with the queen casually resting her elbow on his knee.[95]

The harmony of the couple in the garden of Eden was shattered when the wife was rash enough to accept the suggestion of the rather tame and much-demythologized serpent that she should infringe the Divine Order by eating from the 'tree of the knowledge of good and evil'.[96] This enigmatic intrusion into the orchard has been much discussed, but it probably stands for nothing more esoteric than the concept of law and order. Significantly, it is the scribal literature of Solomon's age which provides the necessary clues. David is said by the woman of Tekoah to be 'like the angel of God', because he 'can decide between *good* and *evil*' and 'knows all that goes on in the land'. This language echoes the flattery offered to the Pharaoh as the supreme fount of justice.[97] Similarly, Solomon prayed for 'a heart with skill to listen' in order to 'distinguish *good* from *evil*'.[98] The legal background of this terminology is confirmed when the Yahwist represents Laban as saying that the question of Rebecca's marriage is out of his hands ('we cannot speak to you *evil* or *good'*), because God has already given his decision,[99] as, later in the narrative, Laban is forbidden to take legal action against Jacob: 'Be careful to say nothing to Jacob, either *good* or *evil*.'[100] In the light of this usage, to take the forbidden fruit of the 'tree of the knowledge of good and evil' means to take the law into one's own hands and arrogate to oneself the authority which belongs to God alone. 'Do not discover for thy own self the will of God,' warns Amenemope and man's obligation to accept the divinely-determined Order (*ma 'at*) is fundamental teaching in all the scribal literature.[101] Finally, the writer's choice of manual labour as the penalty for man's attempt to become independent of the Creator – 'you shall gain your bread by the sweat of your brow' – may not be unconnected with the scribes' explicit repugnance for it.[102]

However much we allow for the Yahwist's personal insight, it is entirely congruous with his scribal milieu that man's assumption of autonomy should awaken a sense of shame[103] and that this sense of shame should be so closely connected with sex.[104] Whereas guilt commonly presupposes a single commanding father-figure, shame comes to the fore in relation to what the neighbours think, and their opinions embody authority in a more diffused and ambiguous way. Shame is the characteristic neurosis of a society which has its eye on public acceptance, reputation and success and, therefore, attaches paramount importance to keeping up appearances. Such craving for recognition was the least fortunate, if not the least effective, contribution made by Egypt's scribal bureaucracy to Solomon's emergent nation and it is reflected not only in the literature of his own age but in writings as distant and diverse as Deuteronomy and the book of Ezekiel.[105]

CHAPTER SEVEN

Solomon's cultural milieu

ANY HISTORICAL reconstruction based exclusively on direct evidence will inevitably be dull and almost certainly erroneous. Only informed speculation about the shape and size of those piece of the jig-saw of the past which are now lost can prevent our misplacing and misinterpreting the sections which survive. This hazardous enterprise is clearly demanded by the immense gaps in our knowledge of the complex cultural interconnections of the eastern Mediterranean in the Late Bronze and Early Iron Ages (1550–900 BC). Until, for example, the discovery in 1928 of the Ras Shamra texts from ancient Ugarit, Canaanite literature was scarcely more than a hypothesis and Canaanite culture a phenomenon merely glimpsed in fragmentary and distorted traditions.[1] Archaeology has filled some of the lacunae, but many remain.

LITERATURE

It is particularly ironic that the Phoenicians, who through the Greeks gave the West its alphabet, are now represented in literature merely by a corpus of stereotyped inscriptions. The recent demonstration that these pedestrian remains are echoed linguistically in a work of genius like the book of Job is supremely tantalizing to the student of the writings of Solomon's age, since it suggests the possibility that they too were indebted to a Phoenician literature now wholly lost to view.[2] This piece of the jig-saw must be supplied by speculation, unless we are prepared to accept such a confident assertion as: 'There can no longer be any doubt that the Bible has preserved some of the best in Phoenician literature, especially lyric and gnomic poetry. . . . Through the Bible the entire civilized world has fallen heir to Phoenician literary art.'[3]

To acknowledge the possibility that the scribes of Solomon's court were indebted to Phoenicia for its literature no less than for its timber and technicians is not necessarily to abandon the hypothesis that they were primarily heirs to the classical tradition of Egypt. Byblos, for example, whose master builders are said to have worked with the men of Tyre on Solomon's Temple,[4] was dominated by Egyptian civilization from the very beginning of its history in the third millennium B C. One of the earliest Egyptian tales, the *Story of Sinuhe* (*c.* 1960 B C), recounts how enthusiastically this courtier was received in the region east of Byblos, just as the wretched Wenamun, in the last major Egyptian source to mention the city, hoped (but failed) to be nearly a thousand years later. Sinuhe during his Syrian exploits made himself understood in his native Egyptian and Wenamun conducted his protracted negotiations with the prince of Byblos without the aid of an interpreter. It has even been suggested that Egyptian scribes may have been employed at Byblos, as (on the evidence of the Amarna letters) they most probably were at Tyre.[5] There is, in addition, abundant archaeological evidence to confirm the cultural debt of Byblos to Egypt, which Wenamun represents its otherwise arrogant ruler as freely acknowledging: 'True, Amun fitted out all the lands. He fitted them out having earlier fitted out the land of Egypt whence you have come. And craftsmanship came forth from it reaching to the place where I am. And learning came forth from it reaching to the place where I am.'[6]

It is evident that the cosmopolitan literary culture of the eastern Mediterranean in the second millennium B C was made possible by the immense seriousness with which the professional scribes embarked on the study of languages. The archives of Ugarit, written in no less than seven languages, contain numerous lexicographical tablets and clear evidence that some of the letters received from abroad were translated into the vernacular for easy reference. Similarly,

Egyptian–Akkadian glossaries were excavated at Tell el-Amarna, where the tablets included copies of Akkadian mythological texts marked in a way which suggests that they were exercises used to instruct Egyptian scribes in cuneiform. The echoes of Canaanite myths in such Egyptian writings as *Astarte and the Tribute of the Sea* and the *Tale of the Two Brothers* are best explained by postulating the Egyptian scribes' ability to read Canaanite dialects.[7] It was such a skill that Hori paraded in his famous *Satirical Letter*.[8] Although the *Instruction of Ani* makes the chauvinistic claim that 'Negroes are taught to speak Egyptian, and Syrians, and all strangers likewise',[9] learning languages was reciprocal in scribal circles.

In the light of this complex literary interchange, what emerges as the most probable hypothesis to account for the compositions of Solomon's scribes? If their affinity with Egyptian literature were simply a matter of style, its mediation through lost Canaanite–Phoenician writings would clearly provide the simplest explanation. At least, some such intermediary must be postulated to account for the connection between the texts of ancient Ugarit and the literature of Israel some four centuries and more later.[10] The affiliation of the Solomonic writings with Egyptian tradition extends, however, beyond a common literary style. The book of Proverbs has been seen to draw directly on a specific and comparatively recent Egyptian composition,[11] and an undoubted knowledge of Egyptian society is found both in the Joseph Story and in the Yahwist's History. It is less easy, although, of course, not impossible, to account for such specifically Egyptian features by appealing to the mediation of Canaanite literature. Since the biblical writers' command of the Hebrew language virtually rules out the possibility that they were bilingual Egyptian scribes, whom Solomon had introduced to his court, as Abi-milki had introduced Egyptian scribes to the court of Tyre, it is probable that they were Hebrews, who had been taught Egyptian.

This conclusion is supported by two further considerations. First, although the authors of the Joseph Story and the

Yahwist's History possess a definite knowledge of things Egyptian, it is an imperfect *outsider's* knowledge.[12] Second, it was a well-established practice from the period of the Middle Kingdom for the Pharaohs to employ Syrians in administrative posts both at home and abroad.[13] For example, two of the Egyptian governors stationed at Gaza, the capital of the province of Canaan during the period covered by the Amarna letters, bore Syrian names and there is a preponderance of non-Egyptian names among their subordinate officers.[14] Also, it is evident that the Egyptian administrators had great confidence in the education of foreigners as a means of establishing their influence abroad, since, from the reign of Tuthmosis III, the young sons and heirs of Syrian vassal kings were brought to the Egyptian court, just as in more spacious days the sons of rajahs were brought to Harrow and Sandhurst, to receive the kind of schooling calculated to equip them for their future responsibilities. One such vassal, writing to protest his loyalty to the Pharaoh, recalls his early life at the Egyptian court:

And although one brick should move from under another, I will not move from under the feet of the king, my lord. So let the king, my lord, ask Iankhamu, his deputy. When I was small, he brought me to Egypt, and I have served the king, my lord, and I have stood in the gate of the king, my lord.[15]

Whether Solomon's scribes had themselves been educated in Egypt, or whether they were simply the pupils of Egyptian-speaking officials living in Palestine, it is impossible to decide, but such evidence as we have, both of the two literatures and of the educational and scribal links between the two countries, points to a direct, rather than a mediated relationship.

ARTS AND CRAFTS
The opposite conclusion must be drawn for most of the non-literary culture of Solomon's kingdom – the product of those arts and crafts which for centuries had been an inseparable adjunct of the pretentious opulence of the courts of the

Ancient Near East. The Amarna letters are pathetically full of megalomaniacal pleas for gifts of gold and of inventories of presents, as expensive as they were useless, which passed to and from the Egyptian court. Thus, we find: 'one bed of ebony, overlaid with ivory and gold', 'five caskets of gold, on whose covers are grapes', 'three hundred [and] seventy-five oil-vessels of ivory', 'one pair of shoes of sheepskin, and covered with pearls of gold', 'one [instrument] for catching flies, whose fingers are trimmed with beautiful, curved *lapis lazuli*', 'one mirror of silver, forty shekels in weight, whose handle is a female statue', and so on *ad nauseam*.[16] With so much international traffic in *objets d'art*, it is hardly surprising that there developed a cosmopolitan 'royal style' and that the opportunist craftsmen of Phoenicia exploited energetically so extensive and lucrative a market. It is doubtful, however, whether the Phoenicians themselves contributed anything more than their incomparable technical skill. Throughout the second millennium B C, the eastern Mediterranean was entirely dominated by the style of Egyptian artists, and it was primarily this which the masons, carvers and metalworkers of Phoenicia imitated, adapted, commercialized and so often failed to comprehend.

Solomon's Jerusalem and his provincial royal cities were almost certainly designed and executed by Phoenicians in this derivative style. The Annals declare explicitly that in Jerusalem 'Solomon's and Hiram's builders and the Gebalites [men of Byblos] shaped the blocks and prepared both timber and stone for the building of the house', and that 'Solomon fetched from Tyre Hiram, the son of a widow of the tribe of Naphtali. His father, a native of Tyre, had been a worker in bronze, and he himself was a man of great skill and ingenuity, versed in every kind of craftsmanship in bronze. Hiram came to King Solomon and executed all his works.'[17] Although there is little possibility that these statements will ever be verified archaeologically in Jerusalem, the excavation of the royal city of Samaria, built for Omri and Ahab some eighty years later than Solomon's capital, has confirmed their reliability to a degree surpassing all expectation.

The Omri family, it is relevant to recall, enjoyed close relations with Phoenicia and Ahab married the notorious Jezebel, daughter of the king of Tyre.[18] His new buildings in Samaria reflected the cultural tradition of his wife. Their masonry was meticulous in its workmanship and, more specifically, included bossed foundation stones of a distinctive type which has been identified in Solomon's Megiddo and traced back to thirteenth-century Ugarit.[19] This evidence from Samaria would not necessarily throw any light on the style of Solomon's architecture in Jerusalem, were it not also for the discovery in Samaria of a deposit of ivories, similarly of Ahab's time. These magnificent pieces confirm the authenticity of the biblical reference to 'the ivory house which he made',[20] and, by comparison with caches of ivories excavated at Megiddo, Arslan Tash and Nimrud, they also confirm the view that Ahab's craftsmen were working in a Phoenician stylistic tradition. As we have seen, these same ivories provide numerous convincing illustrations of the decoration and fittings of the temple as they are described in the Annals.[21] The literary evidence for the King's Works in Jerusalem harmonizes so well with the archaeological evidence for the King's Works in Samaria that the one may be taken as a reliable guide to the other and both used to reconstruct the pervasive but elusive tradition of design which Phoenician enterprise promoted in the Iron Age as a status symbol for the *nouveaux riches*.

GOVERNMENT AND ADMINISTRATION

Israel's adoption of 'a king like all the nations' is often taken to mean that Solomon modelled his new constitution on that of the Canaanite city-states, which had been established in great number throughout Syria and Palestine in the second millennium BC. It has been demonstrated, for example, that the denunciation of kingship ascribed to Samuel need not, as literary critics have long maintained, reflect later experience of Solomon's régime, since the semi-feudal society it depicts had been familiar in Syria from the eighteenth century BC and may now be documented from the archives of Alalakh and Ugarit.[22] These texts certainly establish that the creation of a military aristocracy, the expropriation of land and the granting of fiefs to favoured officials, the exaction of taxes and the exploitation of forced labour, so far from being the diabolical invention of Solomon, were well-established features of royal absolutism throughout the Ancient Near East. They do not, however, settle the complicated question as to whether Solomon was primarily indebted to Canaanite or Egyptian models for his government and administration.

In the period of the New Kingdom, the Pharaohs' rule of their Asiatic empire was significantly different from the control they exercised over their Nubian possessions. As a primitive tribal society, Nubia readily became a colony under direct Egyptian rule and was administered by a viceroy with the help of a separate military commander. Syria, on the contrary, was the home of a mature civilization and its city-states were ruled by hereditary kings no less proud of their cultural tradition than the Pharaohs themselves. Egypt had the wisdom to recognize this difference and made no attempt to impose direct colonial rule on its northern possessions. The Canaanite kings were allowed to retain their thrones on condition that they submitted to vassal treaties which bound them in personal obedience to the Pharaoh. Despite the formal humiliation which this status entailed ('seven times on the belly and seven times on the back' was the salutation expected by the Pharaoh), the vassal kings were, in fact, permitted a considerable degree of independence and continued to recruit their own armies, engage in their petty wars and even reduce their royal neighbours to vassaldom. For example, the ruler of Hazor, remembered in biblical tradition as having been 'formerly the head of all these kingdoms', was powerful and confident enough, when writing to the Pharaoh, to call himself 'King of the city of Hazor', an impertinence without parallel in the other Amarna letters.[23] The activities of these dynasts was controlled only by the

Pharaoh's resident Overseer, who in Palestine, the southern-most of the three provinces into which Egypt's northern territories were divided, made Gaza his headquarters. His main functions were to keep the peace, supervise the payment of tribute and keep in touch with the Bureau for the Corres-pondence of the Pharaoh, that is to say, the Egyptian Colonial Office.

Since it is evident that the Pharaohs never made any attempt to impose their own complex administrative system on the Canaanite city-states, it is difficult to maintain that Solomon's Egyptian-style bureaucracy was derived indirect-ly through his knowledge of them. This is not to deny that many city-states were deeply influenced by their contact with the Egyptian administration. As we have seen, the heirs of some of the vassal kings were actually educated in Egypt and others undoubtedly cultivated the manners and methods of the suzerain power. The rulers of Byblos, for example, had traditionally surrounded themselves with Egyptian jewellery, grandly used hieroglyphs and had their names inscribed in cartouches after the manner of the Pharaohs and yet, at the same time, they called themselves 'governors' as though they were merely Egyptian officials.[24] It is not surprising to learn from the *Journey of Wenamun* that the king of Byblos had a 'letter scribe' and an administrative system efficient enough to produce files about earlier business transactions at a moment's notice.[25] The Phoenician cities, however, were probably unrepresentative in their imitation of things Egypt-ian and, with the exception of those from Tyre, it is significant that no trace of Egyptian influence has been found in the language of the letters from the vassal kings of Palestine in the Amarna archives. Their scribes' 'diplomatic' Akkadian is said to be so full of vernacular Canaanite expres-sions as to discourage any notion that these men were highly-educated and employed by a sophisticated bureaucracy designed on the Egyptian model.[26]

Of all the Canaanite city-states known to have taken part in the Amarna correspondence, Jerusalem offers itself as the obvious clue to that continuity with Egyptian culture and institutions which Solomon's régime so clearly discloses. For centuries, the city resisted conquest, until David succeeded in penetrating what recent excavations have revealed to be the massive walls of the Bronze Age Jebusite fortress.[27] The possibility of a cultural link would be further strengthened if, as some scholars suppose, Jerusalem retained its independent status as a city-state even after it had passed into Israelite possession. However, the six letters sent to the Pharaoh by Abdiheba, king of Jerusalem in the middle of the fourteenth century BC, considerably reduce the hope of our finding here the answer to our problem. So far from disclosing a confident and sophisticated régime, these letters portray a harassed little ruler struggling against overwhelming odds to hold the fort for his Egyptian overlord and pleading repeatedly for military reinforcements. He is even reduced to begging the Egyptian authorities to make sure that his palace is strong enough to withstand burglars, since his life had recently been threatened when the Pharaoh's unpaid and ravenous mercenaries broke in through the roof.[28] The only probable legacy of Canaanite Jerusalem to the age of Solomon was, as we have seen, theological rather than constitutional, and this legacy included the idea that the Israelite king was the anointed vassal of Yahweh, just as his Jebusite predecessors were the anointed vassals of the Pharaoh.[29]

Archaeological indications confirm the evidence of the Amarna letters that in size and structure the Syrian city-states provide inadequate prototypes for Solomon's emergent nation. Even the exceptionally large and important kingdom of Ugarit with all its outlying territories was at most forty miles square, and the kingdoms of Tyre, Sidon, Berytus and Byblos succeeded each other on a coastal strip no more than sixty miles long.[30] Such data help explain why, in the Amarna letters, when the Syrian kings make urgent appeals to the Pharaoh for troops, they usually mention quite trivial numbers like ten, twenty, thirty and fifty men.[31] By contrast, Solomon ruled a nation estimated at nearly a quarter of a million and 'from Dan to Beer-sheba' (as the crow flies) it is no less than 160 miles.

Nor does the political structure of the Syrian city-states afford any convincing analogy for Solomon's kingdom. Whereas the city-states and their people took their name from the city, which, with its surrounding villages, in fact *was* the kingdom, Solomon's national state took its name from the people, whose identity was quite independent of its occupation of a particular territory. In addition, the city-states of Syria, while sometimes extending their power through a system of vassalage, showed no inclination to expand by the absorption of their neighbours, whereas the Israelite kingdom, like other national states, came into being by military conquest and the integration of new territories into a unified political structure.

Although the powerful kingdom of Hazor in its heyday came near to constituting an exception to this general rule (significantly, Jabin, in the biblical record, is referred to as 'the King of Canaan'), it cannot have given a lead to emergent Israel, since it was destroyed by fire (and probably by Israelites) in the second half of the thirteenth century BC and remained, until Solomon rebuilt it as a royal city, merely a settlement of semi-nomadic people without walls or public buildings.[32] Other strongholds of Canaanite civilization suffered a comparable fate at about the same time. Ugarit was overwhelmed by the 'Peoples of the Sea' at the height of its prosperity about 1234 BC and abandoned to a population which could not even read its alphabetic script. Lachish, which had flourished since 1550 BC as an important centre for the Egyptian administration in Palestine, was burnt to the ground about 1200 BC and left virtually deserted for more than a century. Gaza, at one time the capital of the Egyptian province of Canaan, remained, probably, outside Israel's reach, both before and after it was occupied by the Philistines. Megiddo, a sophisticated Bronze Age city, as attested by excavation and the list of loot recorded after its capture by Tuthmosis III in 1481 BC, was reduced to ruins in the middle of the twelfth century B C and remained sunk in obscurity until Solomon once again brought it into promin- ence as one of his royal cities.[33] Gezer, the third of Solomon's royal cities, was one of the few Canaanite strongholds which survived until the establishment of the Hebrew monarchy, when it was captured by Egypt and given to Solomon as a dowry on his marriage to the Pharaoh's daughter. Further excavations at Gezer since 1967 have revealed little to suggest that it was ever a major enclave of Canaanite culture and have established that for a period it was in the hands of the Philistines.[34] Gezer makes its contribution to our problem not by supplying the missing link between Canaanite culture and the Solomonic developments, but by pointing to the alternative hypothesis – that in the sphere of government and administration Solomon depended on his direct contacts with the Egyptian court.

The Pharaoh's annexation of Gezer in the tenth century B C is not a wholly isolated example of Egypt's continuing in- fluence in Palestine even after the loss of its Asiatic posses- sions following the death of Ramesses III. Totally unexpected evidence for it has emerged from a re-examination of the archaeological data of Beth-Shean, the northern fortress and trading centre twelve miles south of the Sea of Galilee, which was excavated some fifty years ago.[35] It appears that in the twelfth century B C, Ramesses III, as part of a new aggressive foreign policy, developed the city as the H.Q. of his Northern Command and posted there one Ramesses Weser-Khepesh, who rejoiced in the titles 'Overseer of Soldiers, Commander of the bowmen of the Lord of the Two Lands, Royal Scribe and Great Steward'. So much we learn from the stone-cut hieroglyphic inscriptions discovered on door-jambs and lin- tels of his official residence. The plan of this splendid house and a number of distinctive building forms establish that it was the work of an Egyptian architect.[36] Next to the house stood a small but complex temple about fifty feet square, resembling in lay-out shrines excavated at Tell el-Amarna, and almost certainly the centre of a hybrid cult of Canaanite

44, 45 The two sides of an ivory panel (100 × 50 cm.) from a bed in the palace of Ugarit, *c.* 1400 BC. The upper illustration (the inner side of the panel) depicts the *private* life of the king in six plaques, between sacred trees at each end. From left to right, the scenes show (1) a man making an offering; (2) a huntsman; (3) a young princess holding a stylized 'lotus' sceptre; (4) two figures being suckled by the mother-goddess; (5) the king and queen caressing; (6) a court official dressed in the Egyptian style. The lower illustration (the outer side of the panel) depicts the *public* life of the king in its six plaques. From left to right, the scenes show (1) a nude fertility goddess holding the Egyptian *ankh* symbol; (2) the king hunting a lion; (3) the king slaying an enemy (4) two army officers; (5) a huntsman carrying a lion; (6) a courtier dressed in Egyptian style.

46 Limestone relief (height 53 cm.) from the tomb of Horemheb at Saqqara (Dynasty XVIII). It depicts six full-bearded Syrians, two Libyans with pointed beards and a clean-shaven (?) Negro, as they grovel on the belly and the back before Horemheb.

47 Seal of an Egyptian official from Megiddo, with the inscription 'head of the bureau of the cattle census, Yufseneb'. The name is quite common but occurs only during the Middle Kingdom, especially in Dynasty XII.

48, 49   Back and front of an ivory wand from Megiddo, found in the stratum of Dynasty XVIII, but possibly considerably older. It is a rare Palestinian example of the 'magic wands' of ivory associated primarily with Egypt during the Middle Kingdom. The inscription invokes magical protection over a lady of the house whose name appears to be non-Egyptian.

50   Gold-mounted obsidian casket (length 4·5 cm.; width 2·3 cm.; height 2·2 cm.) from a royal tomb at Byblos (Dynasty XII). An inscription in a cartouche on the lid records the throne-name of Ammenemes IV.

51   Fragments of a limestone lintel (143 × 50 × 21 cm.) from Beth-Shean (Dynasty XX). They were probably part of a doorway in the official residence of Ramesses Weser-Khepesh. On the right, a worshipping figure adores the cartouches of the reigning king, Ramesses III.

52   Upper part of basalt stela (height 242 cm.) of Sethos I (1318–1304 BC) from the first year of his reign found at Beth-Shean (Dynasty XIX). The king (on the left) is making offerings to Re-Harakhty, the god in the form of a falcon crowned with the solar disc. The inscription recounts how Sethos I campaigned in northern Palestine against a coalition of Asiatic princes.

53   Upper part of basalt stela (height 267 cm.) of Ramesses II (1304–1237 BC) from the ninth year of his reign found at Beth-Shean (Dynasty XIX). The king (on the right) raises his hand in a gesture of address to the god Amon-Re, crowned with double plumes. The inscription recounts how Ramesses II was victorious over the Asiatics.

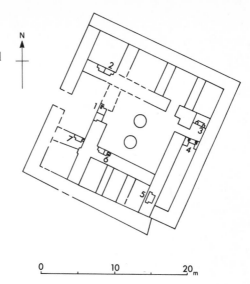

Fig. 27   Plan of the house (excavation number 1500) at Beth-Shean. The central columned hall surrounded by smaller rooms is a distinctive feature of Egyptian houses and is found at Amarna and in the Ramesside village of Deir el-Medina.

and Egyptian gods.[37] To complete the cultural mix, anthropoid coffins on the site suggest (in the absence of Philistine pottery) that the troops garrisoned there by the Egyptians were Aegean mercenaries.[38]

However, the astonishing feature of the Beth-Shean story is the survival of the Egyptian presence there long after the death of Ramesses III. It has been demonstrated, for example, that such symbols of Egyptian allegiance as the stelae of Sethos I and Ramesses II, with a statue of Ramesses III, were rescued when Beth-Shean was destroyed about 1075 BC and devotedly set up again after the city's restoration. The fact that these monuments were discovered with pottery of the period 950–900 BC implies that Egyptian influence at Beth-Shean was tolerated throughout David's reign and survived until the city was absorbed into Solomon's regional administration. In discussing the reasons for this unexpected situation, the scholar who has recently reviewed the archaeological data observes: 'It has even been suggested that David's administration was modelled on the Egyptian, and that royal scribes were imported from the land of the Nile by both David and Solomon.'[39]

A similar conclusion is supported, as we have seen, by the literature of Solomon's age. It is further confirmed by additional biblical evidence of a direct and lively relationship between Israel and Egypt in the early years of the monarchy. This testimony is sufficiently explicit to cast doubt on more tortuous and ingenious hypotheses to account for the Egyptian style of Solomon's government. The vivid little narrative of Hadad's escape from Edom to the Pharaoh's court, where he was given not only political asylum but the honour of the queen's sister as a bride, clearly suggests the survival at this period of Egypt's traditional relations with Palestine.[40] Although in its present context the story has been exploited by the editor to account for the disruption and decline of the kingdom after Solomon's death, its detail illustrates that his scribes were well acquainted with life at the Egyptian court.

More significant, however, is the biblical record of another marriage alliance with an unnamed pharaoh of the Twenty-first Dynasty: 'Solomon allied himself to Pharaoh king of Egypt by marrying his daughter.' That this arrangement was regarded as effecting more than a casual accession to the royal harim is indicated by the special house which Solomon ordered to be built for his Egyptian wife, and by the scribal note that Gezer came into Israelite possession as her dowry.[41] In the Amarna letters, when one of the kings of Babylon was rash enough to ask for the hand of the Pharaoh's daughter, he was given a distinctly dusty answer: 'From of old, a daughter of the King of Egypt has not been given to anyone.' It has recently been argued that Solomon's privilege was, indeed, wholly without precedent.[42] This indication of Solomon's standing in relation to Egypt in the period of its disintegration is confirmed by the probability that the Pharaoh (?Siamun), having conquered Gezer in a minor military expedition, was later compelled to cede the city to Solomon.[43] Egypt had now met its match and the only recognition it could look for from Solomon's emergent nation was the flattery of wholesale imitation.

Notes to the text

ABBREVIATIONS

A.N.E.P.   J. B. Pritchard, *The Ancient Near East in pictures relating to the Old Testament* (2nd ed., 1969)

A.N.E.T.   J. B. Pritchard, *Ancient Near Eastern Texts relating to the Old Testament* (2nd ed., 1955)

B.A.   *The Biblical Archaeologist*

B.A.R.   J. H. Breasted, *Ancient Records of Egypt* (5 vols, 1906)

B.A.S.O.R.   *Bulletin of the American Schools of Oriental Research*

B.J.R.L.   *Bulletin of the John Rylands Library*

C.A.H.   *The Cambridge Ancient History* (Revised edition, vols I, II, with page references as in the original fascicles)

C.E.   *Chronique d'Égypte*

D.O.T.T.   D. Winton Thomas (ed.), *Documents from Old Testament Times* (1958)

E.A.   El-Amarna Letters, J. Knudtzon, *Die El-Amarna-Tafeln* (1907–15); S. A. B. Mercer, *The Tell El-Amarna Tablets* (1939) provides an English translation

Erman, A. E.   Adolf Erman, *The Ancient Egyptians* (trans. A. M. Blackman), with introduction by W. K. Simpson (1966)

E.T.   *Expository Times*

I.E.J.   *Israel Exploration Journal*

J.B.L.   *Journal of Biblical Literature*

J.E.A.   *Journal of Egyptian Archaeology*

J.N.E.S.	*Journal of Near Eastern Studies*
J.T.S.	*Journal of Theological Studies*
L.E.M.	R. A. Caminos, *Late-Egyptian Miscellanies* (1954), a translation with commentary of A. H.

	Gardiner, *Late-Egyptian Miscellanies* (1937)
P.E.Q.	*Palestine Exploration Quarterly*
R.B.	*Revue Biblique*
V.T.	*Vetus Testamentum*

1 THE ANNALS OF SOLOMON

1 I Kgs. 16.15–28.

2 I Kgs. 16.29–22.40.

3 I Kgs. 11.41; cf. J. Liver, 'The Book of the Acts of Solomon', *Biblica*, 48 (1967), pp. 75–101.

4 I Kgs. 3.1–3; 6.1, 11–14; 7.48–51; 8.1–9.9; 9.25; 11.1–43.

5 I Kgs. 3.9–12; cf. 3.28.

6 I Kgs. 10.4–8.

7 I Kgs. 5.7, 12.

8 I Kgs. 4.29–34.

9 I Kgs. 7.14; I Chron. 22.15; II Chron. 2.7; Jer. 10.9; Ezek. 27.8, 9; Exod. 28.3; 31.3–6; 35.26–36.1.

10 II Sam. 14.20; I Kgs. 3.12, 28; 4.29–34; 5.7, 12; 10.1–25; 11.41; II Chron. 1.10–12; Isa. 10.13; 11.2.

11 I Kgs. 2.6, 9; Isa. 19.11; 29.14; Jer. 50.35; Prov.

16.14; cf. Gen. 41.33, 39; Deut. 1.13–15.

12 Jer. 10.7, 12; 51.15; Prov. 3.19; Ps. 104.24; Job 9.4; 11.6; 12.13; 15.8; cf. Isa. 31.2.

13 Ezek. 28.4, 5.

14 I Kgs. 4.34; 10.1.

15 See pp. 165–66.

16 *B.A.R.*, II, § 867; cf. William C. Hayes, *C.A.H.*, vol. II, chap. IX, part 1 (1962), pp. 28–36.

17 *B.A.R.*, II, § 869.

18 I Kgs. 10.4, 5.

19 I Kgs. 10.3, 8.

20 See pp. 112–14.

21 Job 28.1–28; 42.3; Ecclus. 11.4; Ps. 139.6; cf. Deut. 30.11–14.

22 I Kgs. 10.9.

23 I Kgs. 3.4–15; cf. 3.28.

24 Deut. 1.9–18; see Moshe

Weinfeld, *Deuteronomy and the Deuteronomic School* (1972), pp. 244–57.

25 *B.A.R.*, II, §§ 810–15; *A.N.E.T.*, p. 449; cf. R. N. Whybray, *The Succession Narrative* (1968), pp. 100–101.

26 I Kgs. 3.11.

27 *B.A.R.*, III, §§ 394–414.

28 *B.A.R.*, III, § 402.

29 I Kgs. 3.9; *A.N.E.T.*, p. 414*a*; Erman, *A.E.*, p. 64; see pp.

30 *B.A.R.*, II, § 676; cf. § 680; to 'go in and go out' was so well-established an idiom as to be used of the Netherworld, cf. *B.A.R.*, IV, §§ 187, 382.

31 *B.A.R.*, III, § 400.

32 See p. 139.

33 Exod. 3.7–4.12; Jer. 1.4–10.

34 I Kgs. 3.16–28; cf. T. H. Gaster, *Myth, Legend and Custom in the Old Testament* (1969), pp. 491–94.

35 Prov. 2.16–19; 7.1–27; 9.13–18; 23.26–28; 29.3; see pp.

36 II Sam. 14.4–20.

37 I Kgs. 3.28.

38 *B.A.R.*, II, § 768.

39 *B.A.R.*, IV, § 246.

40 *B.A.R.*, IV, § 402; cf. § 266.

41 *B.A.R.*, IV, §§ 423, 426; *A.N.E.T.*, pp. 214–16; cf. I Kgs. 4.1–19.

42 *B.A.R.*, IV, § 466; cf. J. Černý, *C.A.H.*, vol. II, chap. XXXV (1965), pp. 5–6.

43 I Kgs. 5.15–17.

44 I Kgs. 6.2–7.47; cf. *B.A.R.*, IV, §§ 189, 191, 199, 201, 203.

45 I Kgs. 7.47.

46 I Kgs. 10.20; cf. *B.A.R.*, II, § 158.

47 I Kgs. 10.27.

48 *B.A.R.*, IV, §§ 190, 216, 217; cf. §§ 210, 213, 409.

49 *B.A.R.*, II, §§ 884, 990, 992, 1002; III, § 404.

50 I Kgs. 4.29; 4.20, 21; cf. 4.25; 5.4.

51 *B.A.R.*, IV, §§ 188, 410; cf. §§ 246, 401; II, §§ 804, 887, 992; *A.N.E.T.*, pp. 260, 378; Erman, *A. E.*, p. 277.

52 I Kgs. 9.26–28; *B.A.R.*, II, §§ 246–95; IV, § 407; see p. 25.

53 I Kgs. 5.1–11; *A.N.E.T.*, pp. 25–29; Erman, *A. E.*, pp. 174–85; *B.A.R.*, IV, §§ 557–91.

54 Alan. H. Gardiner, *Egypt of the Pharaohs* (1961), p. 311.

55 I Kgs. 5.9.

56 Alan H. Gardiner, *op. cit.*, p. 309.

2 THE INHERITANCE OF SOLOMON

1 I Kgs. 4.21.

2 II Sam. 8.3–12; 10.1–19; see A. Malamat, 'The Kingdom of David and Solomon in its contact with Egypt and Aram Naharaim', *B.A.*, XXI.4 (1958), pp. 100–102; B. Mazar, 'The Aramean Empire and its Relations with Israel', *B.A.*, XXV.4 (1962), pp. 102–104.

3 II Sam. 8.2, 13, 14; cf. 12.26–31.

4 II Sam. 5.11; 7.2; cf. I Kgs. 5.1–6.

5 I Sam. 22.2.

6 I Sam. 22.1–23.13; 25.1–28.2; 29.1–11; 31.1–13; II Sam. 1.1–27.

7 II Sam. 2.4; 5.3–10, 17–25.

8 II Sam. 24.1–9; see p. 42; cf. G. Buccellati, *Cities and Nations of Ancient Syria* (1967), pp. 213–15.

9 G. Buccellati, *op. cit.*, pp. 162–68, 179–81, 195–200.

10 I Kgs. 1.32–40; II Sam. 2.8–4.12.

11 R. de Vaux, 'Le roi d'Israël, vassal de Yahvé', *Mélanges Eugène Tisserant*, I (*Studi e Testi* 231), 1964, pp. 119–33, trans. in *The Bible and the Ancient Near East* (1972), pp. 152–66; cf. *Ancient Israel* (1961), pp. 103–105.

12 II Kgs. 11.12.

13 Ps. 18.35–43; cf. Pss. 2.1–5, 8–12; 21.8–12; 47.2, 3; 89.19–27; 110.1, 2; cf. A. Barucq, *L'Expression de la louange divine et de la prière dans la Bible et en Égypte* (1962), pp. 490–96; 500–501; cf. the review by B. Couroyer, *R.B.*, LXXII (1965), pp. 281–86; G. von Rad, 'The Royal Ritual in Judah', *The Problem of the Hexateuch and Other Essays* (1966), pp. 222–31; R. de Vaux, *Ancient Israel* (1961), pp. 108–10.

14 II Sam. 8.15–18; 20.23–26; I Kgs. 4.1–6; see pp. 47–50.

15 R. de Vaux, *Histoire ancienne d'Israël* (1971), p. 470.

16 I Sam. 14.52; 16.14–20; 18.27, 30; II Sam. 15.18; 20.7; 21.15–22; 23.8–23; I Kgs. 1.38, 44; see pp. 55–57. Y. Yadin argues that David's army had at least a small chariot squadron and observes that 'the militia system and the census project make manifest the existence of a very high-level administrative machine in the days of David and Solomon', *The Art of Warfare in Biblical Lands* (1963), pp. 275–87.

17 Josh. 15.1–12; 16.1–8; 17.7–

10; 18.12–20; 19.10–14, 25–29, 33, 34; cf. Y. Aharoni, *The Land of the Bible* (1966), pp. 227–39.

18 II Sam. 2.11; 5.3–5; 24.9; I Kgs. 2.10, 11.

19 II Sam. 19.41–43.

20 II Sam. 20.1, 2; I Kgs. 12.16.

21 Judg. 10.1–5; 12.8–15; cf. O. Eissfeldt, *C.A.H.*, vol. II, chap. XXXIV (1965), pp. 18–20; H.-J. Kraus, *Worship in Israel* (1966), pp. 125–78.

22 G. E. Mendenhall, 'The Hebrew Conquest of Palestine', *B.A.*, XXV.3 (1962), pp. 66–87; cf. R. de Vaux, *Histoire ancienne d'Israël* (1971), pp. 452–54.

23 M. Greenberg, *The Ḫab/piru, American Oriental Series*, 39 (1955), pp. 85–88; 91–96; cf. E. F. Campbell, Jr., 'The Amarna Letters and The Amarna Period', *B.A.*, XXIII.1 (1960), pp. 13–15; R. de Vaux, *op. cit.*, pp. 106–12, 202–208.

24 G. E. Mendenhall, *op. cit.*, p. 74.

25 II Sam. 20.1, 2; I Sam. 8.1–22; 10.17–27; 12.19.

26 II Sam. 7.1–7; see R. de Vaux, 'Jérusalem et les prophètes', *R.B.*, LXXIII (1966), pp. 482–88. It is difficult to follow de Vaux in ascribing II Sam. 7 to

David's reign, even if its relationship to the Egyptian genre of the *Königsnovelle* is accepted; cf. M. Noth, *The Laws in the Pentateuch and Other Essays* (1966), pp. 256–57; D. J. McCarthy, 'II Samuel 7 and the Structure of the Deuteronomic History', *J.B.L.*, LXXXIV (1965), pp. 131–38.

27 Acts 7.44–51; cf. M. Simon, 'Saint Stephen and the Jerusalem Temple', *The Journal of Ecclesiastical History*, II.2 (1951), pp. 127–42.

3 THE NEW BUREAUCRACY

1 II Sam. 8.15–18, cf. 20.23–26; I Kgs. 4.1–6.

2 II Sam. 8.17.

3 II Sam. 20.25.

4 I Kgs. 4.3.

5 A. Cody, 'Le Titre égyptien et le nom propre du scribe de David', *R.B.*, LXXII (1965), pp. 381–93.

6 Cf. Ps. 45.1; Jer. 8.8; 36.32.

7 Tryggve N. D. Mettinger, *Solomonic State Officials* (1971), pp. 7–12.

8 In fact, I Kgs. 4.3 names *two* Secretaries: Elihoreph and Ahijah, the sons of Seraiah, David's Secretary. For one solution to the textual problem, see the New English Bible.

9 II Kgs. 22.3–13; cf. Jer. 36.1–26 and J. Muilenburg, 'Baruch the Scribe', in J. I. Durham and J. R. Porter (ed.), *Proclamation and Presence* (1970), pp. 223–31.

10 II Kgs. 12.4–16.

11 Tryggve N. D. Mettinger, *op. cit.*, pp. 25–51; R. de Vaux, 'Titres et fonctionnaires égyptiens à la cour de David et de Solomon', *R.B.*, XLVIII (1939), pp. 394–405; *Ancient Israel* (1961), pp. 127–32. It should be noted that this interpretation parts company with the New English Bible, which translates *sopher* as 'Adjutant-general' and uses the title 'Secretary of State' for the *mazkir*, called here the 'Royal Herald'.

12 II Kgs. 18.18, 37; cf. *B.A.R.*, II, §§ 763–71.

13 II Kgs. 15.5; Isa. 22.15–22; *B.A.R.*, II, §§ 679–80; selections in *A.N.E.T.*, pp. 212–14; see p. 23.

14 R. de Vaux, *Ancient Israel* (1961), pp. 129–31.

15 William C. Hayes, *C.A.H.*, vol. II, chap. IX, part 1 (1962), p. 50. In addition to the Secretary of State, the Royal Herald and the Steward, the title 'King's Friend' is included in the list of Solomon's officials (I Kgs. 4.5; cf. II Sam. 15.37; 16.16),

after which it disappears. Egyptian models have been claimed both for this office (or rank) and for the 'Thirty', a council of elders which, it is suggested, was instituted to advise the king (II Sam. 23.18–39; I Kgs. 12.6; 20.7, 8). The evidence, however, is far from conclusive: cf. Tryggve N. D. Mettinger, *op. cit.*, pp. 63–69; R. J. Williams in J. R. Harris (ed.), *The Legacy of Egypt* (1971), p. 272; R. de Vaux, *Histoire ancienne d'Israël* (1971), p. 137.

16 For arguments against the view that the city of Jerusalem was the king's personal property, see G. Buccellati, *Cities and Nations of Ancient Syria* (1967), pp. 160–81.

17 I Sam. 8.14; cf. I Sam. 22.7, 8; II Sam. 14.30; I Kgs. 2.26; 21.1–16.

18 Josh. 21.9–42; I Chron 6.54–81; see Y. Aharoni, *The Land of the Bible* (1966), pp. 268–73. For the benefactions of Ramesses III to the temples, see *A.N.E.T.*, pp. 260–62; *B.A.R.*, IV, §§ 151–412.

19 I Kgs. 1.7, 8; 2.26, 35; 4.2. The reference to Zadok and Abiathar in I Kgs. 4.4 may be regarded as an interpolation from David's list (II Sam. 8.17).

20 II Kgs. 4.22, 23. For 'fat-

tened fowl' in Egypt, cf.
B.A.R., IV, §§ 217, 260, 323.

21 I Kgs. 4.7–19, 27; see D. B.
Redford, in J. W. Wevers
and D. B. Redford (ed.),
*Studies on the Ancient Pales-
tinian World* (1972), pp. 144–
56.

22 G. E. Wright, 'The Provinces of Solomon', *Eretz-
Israel*, VIII (1967), pp. 58–
68.

23 Cf. Judg. 1.27–33.

24 I Kgs. 4.9–13.

25 I Kgs. 4.15 (cf. II Sam.
15.27); 4.12 (cf. 4.3); 4.16
(cf. II Sam. 15.32–37).

26 A. R. Johnson, *Sacral Kingship in Ancient Israel* (2nd
ed., 1967), p. 52, n. 1.

27 For a recent discussion of
Solomon's administrative
districts, see Tryggve N. D.
Mettinger, *op. cit.*, pp. 111–
27.

28 I Sam. 8.11–17; see pp.
167–68. For 'cooks and confectioners' in Egypt, cf.
B.A.R., III, § 624.

29 William C. Hayes, *op. cit.*,
p. 47.

30 I Kgs. 4.28; cf. 9.22.

31 William Stevenson Smith,
*Interconnections in the Ancient
Near East* (1965), pp. 22–23.

32 Josh. 17.16–18; Judg. 1.19;
4.13; I Sam. 13.5; II Sam.

1.6; 8.4; cf. Josh. 11.1–9.

33 I Kgs. 10.26; cf. 4.26; 9.15–
19.

34 I Kgs. 10.29; *A.N.E.T.*, pp.
278–79; see p. 66.

35 Despite the New English
Bible: see I Kgs. 4.26; 9.22;
I Sam. 8.11, 12; cf. R. O.
Faulkner, 'Egyptian Milit-
ary Organisation', *J.E.A.*,
XXXIX (1953), p. 43; D. R.
Ap-Thomas in J. I. Durham
and J. R. Porter (ed.), *Pro-
clamation and Presence* (1970),
pp. 135–51.

36 William C. Hayes, *op. cit.*,
pp. 24–26; *A.N.E.T.*, pp.
244–45.

37 A. R. Schulman, 'The
Egyptian Chariotry: a Re-
examination', *Journal of the
American Research Center in
Egypt*, II (1963), pp. 75–98.

38 I Kgs. 4.6. Adoram appears
as holding this office in II
Sam. 20.24, but the reference is suspect; cf. R. de
Vaux, *Ancient Israel* (1961),
pp. 128, 141.

39 I Kgs. 5.13, 14; cf. 15.16–22.

40 *E.A.*, 365; cf. A. F. Rainey,
'Compulsory labour gangs
in ancient Israel', *I.E.J.*,
20.34 (1970), pp. 194–95;
A. F. Rainey, *El Amarna
Tablets 359–379* (1970), pp.
24–27.

41 William C. Hayes, *op. cit.*,
part 2, p. 17.

42 I Kgs. 12.1–19.

43 I Kgs. 11.26–12.20.

44 I Kgs. 9.20–23; cf. Josh. 16.10; Judg. 1.27–35; II Sam. 12.26–31; Deut. 20.11. Even if the terms *mas* and *mas 'obed* are not clearly differentiated, as A. F. Rainey maintains, they appear, nevertheless, to reflect two types of forced labour (see, above, note 40).

45 I Kgs. 5.15, 16; 9.23.

46 J. Černý, *C.A.H.*, vol. II, chap. XXV (1965), pp. 17–23; cf. *B.A.R.*, IV, §§ 461–68.

47 R. A. Caminos, *L.E.M.*, pp. 497–98; see p. 26.

4 THE KING'S WORKS

1 I Kgs. 10.1–13; see E. Ullendorff, 'The Queen of Sheba', *B.J.R.L.*, 45 (1962–63), pp. 486–504.

2 I Kgs. 10.15.

3 Num. 20.17; 21.22; see p. 33.

4 G. W. Van Beek, 'Frankincense and Myrrh', *B.A.*, XXIII.3 (1960), pp. 70–95.

5 I Kgs. 9.18, reading 'Tadmor' for 'Tamar', as in II Chron. 8.4; cf. O. Eissfeldt, *C.A.H.*, vol. II, chap. XXXIV (1965), pp. 56–57.

6 I Kgs. 9.26–28; 10.11, 22.

7 B. Maisler, 'The Excavation of Tell Qasîle', *B.A.*, XIV.2 (1951), pp. 43–49; 'The Excavations at Tell Qasîle', *I.E.J.*, I (1950–51), pp. 61–76, 125–40, 194–218; 'Two Hebrew Ostraca from Tell Qasîle' *J.N.E.S.*, X.4 (1951), pp. 265–67.

8 G. W. Van Beek, *op. cit.*, pp. 75–82; cf. W. Culican, *The First Merchant Venturers* (1966), pp. 77–79; R. D. Barnett, *The Nimrud Ivories* (1957), pp. 59–60, 167–68.

9 I Kgs. 9.12–14; cf. II Chron. 8.1, 2.

10 *A.N.E.T.*, pp. 477–78; Erman, *A. E.*, p. 231; see pp. 112–14.

11 I Kgs. 10.28, 29; cf. *A.N.E.T.*, p. 279a, n. 9; H. Tadmor, 'Que and Musri', *I.E.J.*, 11.3 (1961), pp. 143–50.

12 I Kgs. 9.15; see Kathleen Kenyon, *Royal Cities of the Old Testament* (1971), pp. 36–70.

13 D. Winton Thomas (ed.), *Archaeology and Old Testament Study* (1967), pp. 393, 394, 202, 440; cf. B. Mazar, ''Ein Gev: Excavations in 1961', *I.E.J.*, 14.1–2 (1964), pp. 1–33.

14 Ezek. 40.6–16; see C. G. Howie, 'The East Gate of Ezekiel's Temple Enclosure and the Solomonic Gateway

of Megiddo', *B.A.S.O.R.*, 117 (1950), pp. 13–19; cf. Y. Yadin, 'Solomon's City Wall and Gate at Gezer', *I.E.J.*, 8.2 (1958), pp. 80–86; *Hazor* (1972), pp. 147–49; William G. Denver and others, 'Further Excavations at Gezer 1967–1971'. *B.A.*, XXXIV.4 (1971), pp. 112–17.

15 R. B. Y. Scott, 'Weights and Measures of the Bible', *B.A.*, XXII.2 (1959), p. 26. Scott suggests that the architect was himself Egyptian.

16 Y. Yadin, *Hazor* (1972), pp. 161–64.

17 D. Ussishkin, 'King Solomon's Palace and Building 1723 in Megiddo', *I.E.J.*, 16.3 (1966), pp. 174–86 and 'King Solomon's Palaces', *B.A.*, 36.3 (1973), pp. 78–105; Y. Yadin, *Hazor* (1972), pp. 154–56; see note 24.

18 H. Frankfort, 'The Origin of the Bît Hilani', *Iraq*, XIV (1952), pp. 120–31; *The Art and Architecture of the Ancient Orient* (1970), pp. 253–54, 282–90.

19 I Kgs. 7.6–12.

20 I Kgs. 10.18–20; see pp. 90–92.

21 I Kgs. 7.9, 10; R. S. Lamon and G. M. Shipton, *Megiddo I* (1939), pp. 19–20.

22 I Kgs. 7.2–5; see Th. A.

Busink, *Der Tempel von Jerusalem* (1970), pp. 129–40.

23 I Kgs. 10.17, 21; Isa. 22.8.

24 K. M. Kenyon, *Jerusalem* (1967), p. 59; D. Ussishkin, 'On the Original Position of Two Proto-Ionic Capitals at Megiddo', *I.E.J.*, 20.3–4 (1970), pp. 213–15.

25 D. Harden, *The Phoenicians* (1963), p. 196.

26 I Kgs. 5.1–18; 7.13–46.

27 J. B. Pritchard, as reported in *The Times*, 22 August 1972. The temple was discovered in the ancient city of Sarepta (Zarephath), on the coast mid-way between Tyre and Sidon. Fragments of figurines of Astarte, Horus and Thoth suggest a syncretistic Canaanite cult with a strong Egyptian influence.

28 I Kgs. 6.2–10; see G. R. H. Wright, 'Pre-Israelite Temples in the Land of Canaan', *P.E.Q.*, January–June, 1971, pp. 17–32.

29 Th. A. Busink, *op. cit.*, pp. 558–62.

30 Y. Yadin, *Hazor* (1972), pp. 83–89.

31 Y. Aharoni, in D. Winton Thomas (ed.), *op. cit.*, pp. 395–97; 'Arad: Its Inscriptions and Temple', *B.A.*, XXXI.1 (1968), pp. 18–32;

Y. Yadin, *Hazor* (1972), p. 86, n. 4.

32 I Kgs. 6.16, 17; see Th. A. Busink, *op. cit.*, pp. 197–209.

33 I Kgs. 6.23–28; I Sam. 4.4; II Kgs. 19.15; Ps. 99.1; cf. R. D. Barnett, *op. cit.*, pp. 85–87, 138–42; H. Frankfort, *op. cit.*, pp. 318–19; M. E. L. Mallowan, *Nimrud and its Remains*, I (1966), p. 145.

34 I Kgs. 6.14–18, 29–35.

35 M. E. L. Mallowan, *op. cit.*, II, pp. 471–80.

36 M. E. L. Mallowan, *op. cit.*, II, pp. 483–85.

37 A. Badawy, *A History of Egyptian Architecture: The Empire* (1968), p. 368; see I Kgs. 6.22, 29–35; 7.47–50.

38 I Kgs. 6.3; 7.19; cf. H. Frankfort, *op. cit.*, p. 358; D. Ussishkin, *op. cit.*, note 24.

39 A. Badawy, *op. cit.*, pp. 469–70.

40 I Kgs. 7.15–22; *B.A.R.*, II, §§ 881, 883, 886, 887, 890; *A.N.E.T.*, pp. 375–76; cf. I Kgs. 6.21–35; 10.5.

41 G. Schumacher, *Tel el-Mutesellim* I (1908), frontispiece; cf. M. E. L. Mallowan, *op. cit.*, I, p. 138.

42 I Kgs. 7.23–26.

43 H. Frankfort, *op. cit.*, p. 322;

cf. A. R. Johnson, *Sacral Kingship in Ancient Israel* (2nd ed., 1967), pp. 59–60.

44 I Kgs. 7.27–39.

45 I Kgs. 10.22; cf. II Chron. 9.21; N. Glueck, 'Eziongeber', *B.A.*, XXVIII.3 (1965), pp. 70–79; D. Winton Thomas (ed.), *op. cit.*, pp. 436–39; cf. B. Rothenberg, 'Ancient copper industries in the Western Arabah', *P.E.Q.*, January–June, 1962, pp. 5–71.

46 Isa. 23.1, 5–7, 12; cf. Jer. 10.9.

47 W. Culican, *op. cit.*, pp. 114–16; D. Harden, *op. cit.*, pp. 64, 159–60.

48 H. W. Catling, *C.A.H.*, vol. II, chap. XXII(b) (1966), pp. 70–72.

49 I Kgs. 5.9; B. Maisler, *op. cit.*, see note 7.

50 I Kgs. 7.28, 29, 36.

51 J. B. Pritchard, 'The First Excavations at Tell es-Sa 'idiyeh', *B.A.*, XXVIII.1 (1965), pp. 10–17.

52 I Kgs. 7.45–46.

53 I Kgs. 7.7; 10, 18–20; cf. 7.47.

54 Ps. 99.1.

55 J. Vandier, *Manuel d'Archéologie Égyptienne*, IV (1964), pp. 358–63.

56 I Kgs. 10.19; cf. II Chron. 9.18; Exod. 32.1–8; I Kgs. 12.28; Hos. 8.5, 6; 10.5; 13.2.

57 R. D. Barnett, *op. cit.*, pp. 143–45.

58 H. Frankfort, *op. cit.*, pp. 321–22.

59 Deut. 17.17; I Kgs. 11.1–3.

60 I Kgs. 7.8; 9.24; cf. W. Stevenson Smith, *The Art and Architecture of Ancient Egypt* (1965), pp. 163–64.

61 I Kgs. 10.12; 4.32; II Sam. 19.33–35.

62 H. Frankfort, *op. cit.*, pp. 314–15; M. E. L. Mallowan, *op. cit.*, I, pp. 216–18.

63 J. Vandier, *op. cit.*, pp. 364–90.

64 R. H. Charles, *The Apocrypha and Pseudepigrapha*, vol. II (1913), chaps. 187–300; cf. Otto Eissfeldt, *The Old Testament* (1965), pp. 603–606.

65 I Esdras 3.1–5.3; cf. Otto Eissfeldt, *op. cit.*, pp. 574–76; see p. 143.

66 *A.N.E.T.*, p. 444; Erman, A. E., pp. 110–12; cf. William C. Hayes, *C.A.H.*, vol. I, chap. XX (1961), pp. 33–34.

67 I Kgs. 4.30–33. It is of interest to note that love songs became widely popular in the Nineteenth Dynasty: 'The banquets which were then in vogue provided an opportunity ideally suited to the performance of love songs, perhaps in mime and to a musical accompaniment' (G. Posener, in J. R. Harris (ed.), *The Legacy of Egypt* (1971), pp. 238–39). See Erman, *A. E.*, pp. 242–51.

68 Prov. 30.18, 19; cf. 30.15–16, 21–23.

5 EDUCATION IN WISDOM

1 Ecclus. 51.23.

2 Ecclus. 33. 16; cf. 8.9.

3 Ecclus. 8.8 (trans. *Jerusalem Bible*).

4 Ecclus. 6.32, 33; 14.20, 21; 16.24, 25; 21.18, 19, 21; 21.25, 26.

5 Ecclus. 4.23, 24; 5.8–13; 15.5; 18.29; 21.16, 17; 27.4–7.

6 Ecclus. 1.23, 24; 11.7, 8; 20.7; 20.18–20.

7 Ecclus. 22.7; 33.4, 5.

8 Ecclus. 9.1–9; 19.1–3; 31.25–31; 5.14; 19.5–17; 28.13–26.

9 Ecclus. 13.9–11.

10 Ecclus 31.12–21; 32.1–13.

11 Ecclus. 18.30–33.

12 Ecclus. 7.18–28; 25.13–26. 18; 36.21–26; 40.18–23.

13 Ecclus. 13.2; cf. 4.7; 11.1; 15.5; 20.11; 20.27; 22.23; 23.14; 30.3; 32.10; 37.20, 21; 41.24; 45.3.

14 Ecclus. 50.1–21.

15 Ecclus. 17.11; 19.17; 23.27; 24.23; 35.1.

16 Ecclus. 2.10; 2.15–18; 22.27–23.6; 35.17.

17 Ecclus. 16.24–30; 34.13–17; 39.16–35; 43.1–33; cf. note 46.

18 Ecclus. 33.10–13; cf. 10.4, 5; 10.18.

19 Ecclus. 15.11–20; 37.13–15; 32.23, 24; 4.1–10; 28.1–7; 33.29–31.

20 See notes 59, 71 and 72; also pp. 119–20.

21 Ecclus. 38.24–39.11.

22 Ecclus. 7.15; cf. 6.19.

23 B. van de Walle, 'Le Thème de la satire des métiers dans la littérature égyptienne', *C.E.*, XXII (1947), pp. 50–72; 'L'Humour dans la littérature et dans l'art de l'ancienne Égypte', *Scholae Adriani de Buck memoriae dicatae*, IV (1969), pp. 11–13.

24 S. R. K. Glanville, 'The Instructions of Onchsheshonqy', *Catalogue of Demotic Papyri in the British Museum*, vol. II (1955), column 17, line 23; cf. B. Gemser, 'The Instructions of Onchsheshonqy and Biblical Wisdom Literature', *Supplements to V.T.*, VII (1960), pp. 102–28; William McKane, *Proverbs* (1970), pp. 117–50.

25 B. van de Walle, *La Transmission des textes littéraires égyptiens* (1948), pp. 28–33.

26 *A.N.E.T.*, pp. 432–34; Erman, *A. E.*, pp. 67–72.

27 G. Posener, *Littérature et politique dans l'Égypte de la XIIe dynastie* (1956), pp. 4–8.

28 R. A. Caminos, *L.E.M.*, pp. 371–428. The translator's indications of textual problems have been omitted.

29 Extracts are given in Erman, *A. E.*, pp. 193–97. For an exposition of the privileges of a scribe, see *A.N.E.T.*, pp. 431–32.

30 B. van de Walle, 'Problèmes relatifs aux méthodes d'enseignement dans l'Égypte ancienne', *Les Sagesses du Proche-Orient Ancien*, Bibliothèque des Centres d'Études supérieures spécialisés (1963), pp. 191–207. Also see H. Brunner, *Altägyptische Erziehung* (1957); William C. Hayes, *C.A.H.*, vol. II, chap. IX, part 1 (1962), pp. 52–53.

31 For example, the temple of Ramesses II at Thebes, the so-called 'Ramesseum', the craftsmen's village of Deir

el-Medina near Thebes, and the temple of Ramesses III at Medinet Habu.

32 *A.N.E.T.*, pp. 420–21; Erman, *A. E.*, pp. 234–42; cf. William C. Hayes, *op. cit.*, p. 43.

33 G. Posener, *Littérature et politique dans l'Égypte de la XIIe dynastie* (1956), pp. 4–7 and in B. van de Walle, *La Transmission des textes littéraires égyptiens* (1948), pp. 41–50; also in J. R. Harris (ed.), *The Legacy of Egypt* (1971), pp. 224, 230. A quotation from the *Book of Kemit* occurs at the beginning of the *Satire of the Trades*, *A.N.E.T.*, p. 432*b*, n. 2.

34 See pp. 132–33.

35 R. A. Caminos, *L.E.M.*, pp. 262–63.

36 *Introductory Guide to the Egyptian Collections in the British Museum* (1964), pp. 107–109; G. J. Toomer, in J. R. Harris (ed.), *op. cit.*, pp. 27–45.

37 *A.N.E.T.*, pp. 475–79; Erman, *A.E.*, pp. 214–34.

38 *A.N.E.T.*, p. 476*b*; such knowledge is claimed exclusively for God in Isa. 40.12–14, a passage obviously couched in scribal idiom.

39 See A. F. Rainey, 'The

Soldier-Scribe in *Papyrus Anastasi I*', *J.N.E.S.*, XXVI.1 (1967), pp. 58–60.

40 *A.N.E.T.*, p. 477*a*; the section on arithmetic, omitted from *A.N.E.T.*, is given in Erman, *A.E.*, pp. 223–27.

41 *A.N.E.T.*, p. 475*b*; see pp. 139–42.

42 Alan H. Gardiner, *Ancient Egyptian Onomastica*, vol. I (1947), p. 2*.

43 Alan H. Gardiner, *op. cit.*, p. 37; cf. Erman, *A.E.*, pp. 186–87.

44 I Kgs. 4.33. The present writer does not accept the late date proposed by R. B. Y. Scott, 'Solomon and the Beginnings of Wisdom in Israel', in M. Noth and D. Winton Thomas (ed.), *Wisdom in Israel and in the Ancient Near East, Supplements to V.T.*, III (1960), pp. 262–79.

45 Alan H. Gardiner, *op. cit.*, pp. 6–9, 35.

46 G. von Rad, *The Problem of the Hexateuch and Other Essays* (1966), pp. 281–91. The author finds the influence of *onomastica* in Job 38–39, Ps. 148, Ecclus. 43 and The Song of the Three, vv. 35–68 (*Benedicite*).

47 W. F. Edgerton, 'The Government and the Governed in the Egyptian Empire',

J.N.E.S., VI.3 (1947), pp. 152–60.

48 E. F. Wente, *Late Ramesside Letters* (1967), a translation of J. Černý, *Late Ramesside Letters* (1939).

49 R. A. Caminos, *L.E.M.*, pp. 250–51.

50 *A.N.E.T.*, pp. 412–14; Erman, *A.E.*, pp. 54–56. See J. Leclant, 'Documents nouveaux et points de vue récents sur les sagesses de l'Égypte ancienne', *Les Sagesses du Proche-Orient Ancien, op. cit.*, pp. 5–26.

51 Erman, *A.E.*, pp. 234–42; extracts in *A.N.E.T.*, pp. 420–21.

52 F. Ll. Griffith, *J.E.A.*, XII (1926), pp. 191–231; extracts in *A.N.E.T.*, pp. 421–24. The references follow Griffith's translation, but the quotations are taken from *A.N.E.T.*

53 Isa. 7.1–9; 14.24–27; 28.12; 30.1–5, 15–17; 31.1–3.

54 *Amenemope*, 9.14; 20.1; 22.17.

55 *Amenemope*, 9.11; 21.16.

56 *Amenemope*, 21.5, 6.

57 *Amenemope*, 21.14; cf. 9.5, 6; 10.12–15; 19.13; 23.8–11.

58 *Amenemope*, 22.1–8; cf. 5.1–6.

59 *Amenemope*, 19.16, 17; 20.5,

6; cf. Prov. 16.9; 19.21; 20.24; Thomas à Kempis, *De Imitatione Christi*, i.19; *Ptahhotep*, 115–116; *Ani*, 8.10.

60 *Amenemope*, 19.20.

61 *Amenemope*, 8.11, 12.

62 *Amenemope*, 17.18–19.9.

63 *Amenemope*, 13.15–18; 15.20–16.4; 17.5–14.

64 *Amenemope*, 4.19; 7.16–19; 17.9–12; 17.22–18.1; 18.21–19.1.

65 *Amenemope*, 24.9–14; cf. 4.4–7.

66 *Amenemope*, 26.9–14; cf. 7.15.

67 *Amenemope*, 16.5–10; cf. Luke 16.1–9.

68 *Amenemope*, 1.1–12; 27.16, 17.

69 *Amenemope*, 6.7–12; 7.7–10; 10.10, 11; 22.7, 8; 23.10, 11.

70 *Amenemope*, ·3.13–16; 5.7–14; 22.11–16; 22.20–23.7.

71 *Amenemope*, 23.13–30; 25.1–26.7.

72 *Amenemope*, 19.11–13.

73 *Amenemope*, 9.10–15; 10.10, 11.

74 *Amenemope*, 11.15–20.

75 *Amenemope*, 13.15–18; 23.22–24.7.

76 *Amenemope*, 20.21–21.8.

77 *Amenemope*, 6.14–17; 7.12–15; 8.13–20; 15.20–16.4; 17.18–19.9; 21.9–20.

78 *Amenemope*, 24.22–25.5.

79 *Amenemope*, 9.5–8; 10.6–15; 19.11–20.6; 24.13–20.

80 A reaffirmation of this generally-accepted view of the relationship between the two texts, with a history of the debate since 1924, is given by R. J. Williams, 'The Alleged Semitic Original of the *Wisdom of Amenemope*', *J.E.A.*, 47 (1961), pp. 100–106. Also see B. Couroyer, 'L'Origine égyptienne de la Sagesse d'Amenemopé', *R.B.*, LXX (1963), pp. 208–24.

81 William McKane, *op. cit.*, pp. 22–33, 413–15.

82 The 'instruction' form in Prov. 1–9 is most clearly seen in 1.8–19; 3.1–12; 3.21–35; 4.1–27; 5.1–23; 6.1–5; 6.20–35; 7.1–5; 7.24–27.

83 William McKane, *op. cit.*, pp. 1–10, 373–74.

84 There are references to the Law in Prov. 28.4, 7, 9, but the dogmatic character of the whole chapter, like its pedestrian style, contrasts unambiguously with the rest of the book and discloses its origin in the legal piety of post-exilic Judaism. A further exceptional and

late reference to the Law occurs in Prov. 29.18.

85 Prov. 3.9, 10; cf. *Ani, A.N.E.T.*, p. 420; Erman, *A.E.*, pp. 235, 239.

86 Prov. 15.8; 21.3; 21.27; cf. *Merikare, A.N.E.T.*, p. 417b; Erman, *A.E.*, p. 83; cf. Ecclus. 34.18–26; 35.1–3. On the Egyptian background of the term 'abomination', see Moshe Weinfeld, *Deuteronomy and the Deuteronomic School* (1972), pp. 267–69.

87 Prov. 3.26; 5.21; 15.3; 15.11; 20.12; 20.27; cf. *Ptahhotep, A.N.E.T.*, p. 413a; Erman, *A.E.*, p. 58; *Merikare, A.N.E.T.*, p. 417b; Erman, *A.E.*, p. 83; *Amenemope*, note 66; *Ben Sira*, note 18. See J. Vergote, 'La Notion de Dieu dans les livres de sagesse égyptiens', in *Les Sagesses du Proche-Orient Ancien, op. cit.*, pp. 159–90.

88 Prov. 3.5; 16.3; 16.6; 16.20; 22.19; 29.25; cf. *Amenemope*, notes 58, 69 and 72; *Ben Sira*, note 16.

89 Prov. 15.8; 15.29; 15.33; 18.12; cf. *Ani* (see p. x); *Amenemope*, note 57; also see the Egyptian prayers in *A.N.E.T.*, pp. 379–81 and Erman, *A.E.*, pp. 305–307.

90 Prov. 16.4; 16.33; 19.21; 20.24; 29.26; cf. *Ptahhotep,*

Erman, *A.E.*, p. 57; *Ani, A.N.E.T.*, pp. 420*b*, 421*a*; Erman, *A.E.*, pp. 239, 240; *Amenemope*, note 55.

91 Prov. 2.7, 8; 16.1; 16.9; 21.31; cf. *Amenemope*, note 59.

92 Prov. 2.20–22; 10.3; 10.6; 10.7; 10.9; 10.16; 10.22; 10.24; 10.25; 10.27; 10.28; 10.29; 10.30; 11.4; 11.5; 11.8; 11.18; 11.19; 12.2; 12.7; 12.12; 12.13; 12.21; 12.28; 13.6; 13.9; 13.21; 13.22; 13.25; 14.11; 14.32; 15.6; 16.31; 21.12; cf. *Amenemope*, note 64. The Egyptian preoccupation with life after death significantly disappears from the book of Proverbs, but its concepts of life, death and judgment do not appear to have been integrated with Israelite theology.

93 Prov. 16.2; 17.3; 20.9; 21.2; cf. *Amenemope*, notes 60–63.

94 Prov. 15.27; 17.23; 21.15; 22.12; cf. *Amenemope*, notes 76 and 71; also see the prayers to Amun in R. A. Caminos, *L.E.M.*, pp. 9–10, 50, 56–57; *A.N.E.T.*, p. 380; Erman, *A.E.*, p. 308.

95 Prov. 10.2; 11.1; 11.20; 16.8; 16.11; 19.1; 20.10; 20.23; cf. *Amenemope*, note 77.

96 Prov. 15.25; 16.19; 19.17; 23.10, 11; 28.27; 29.7; cf. *Amenemope*, notes 66 and 67.

97 Prov. 17.5; 22.2; 29.13; cf. *Amenemope*, note 65 and p. 120; *Ben Sira*, note 19.

98 Prov. 20.22; 24.29; 25.21, 22; cf. *Amenemope*, 22.1–8; 5.1–6; 23.8–11.

99 Prov. 10.1; 25.1.

100 R. N. Whybray, *Wisdom in Proverbs* (1965).

101 Prov. 15.21.

102 Prov. 11.16; cf. 13.4.

103 Prov. 12.24; cf. 12.27; 15.19.

104 Prov. 13.8; 14.20; 14.31; 15.25; 16.19; 17.7; 18.23.

105 Prov. 24.21; cf. 25.7.

106 Prov. 13.7.

107 Prov. 15.19.

108 Prov. 20.21.

109 Prov. 13.11.

110 Prov. 6.1–5; 11.15; 17.18; 20.16.

111 Prov. 8.18, 19; 16.16; 22.1; 23.4, 5.

112 Prov. 11.29; 22.26, 27; 24.27.

113 Prov. 10.15.

114 Prov. 24.3, 4; 21.20.

115 Prov. 27.8.

116 Prov. 31.10–31.

117 Prov. 12.4; cf. 31.23; 11.16; 11.22.

118 Prov. 21.9; 25.24; 19.13; 21.19; 27.15, 16.

119 Prov. 19.26; 17.21; 17.25; 20.20; 29.15; 15.20.

120 Prov. 22.6.

121 Prov. 17.2; cf. 28.12; 28.28.

122 Prov. 12.14.

123 Prov. 16.26.

124 Prov. 13.24; 19.18; 20.30; 22.15; 23.13, 14; 29.17.

125 Prov. 4.1–5.

126 Prov. 1.8; 13.1; 15.5; 19.27; 23.22–25.

127 Prov. 1.10–16; 4.14–19; 20.1; 23.19–21; 23.29–35.

128 Prov. 7.1–27; 9.13–18; 23.26–28; 29.3; 31.3.

129 Prov. 2.16–19; 6.20–35; 7.6–23.

130 Prov. 4.25–27.

131 Prov. 5.1–14.

132 Prov. 18.1.

133 Prov. 17.17; 27.10.

134 Prov. 25.16, 17.

135 Prov. 27.6.

136 Prov. 18.24; 19.4; 19.6.

137 Prov. 15.17; 17.1; 21.17.

138 Prov. 15.13; 16.30; 17.22; 18.14.

139 Prov. 4.24; 12.17; 27.2; cf. 8.6–9.

140 Prov. 12.20.

141 Prov. 10.18; 11.13; 16.27, 28; 17.4; 18.8; 20.19; 24.1, 2; 25.8–10; 26.22.

142 Prov. 26.20, 21; 3.30; 17.14; 17.19; 18.19; 20.3.

143 Prov. 25.21, 22; 24.17, 18; 24.28, 29.

144 Prov. 11.24, 25; 14.21; 14.31; 18.5; 22.22; 23.10, 11; 24.11, 12.

145 Prov. 14.8.

146 Prov. 17.8; 18.16; 21.14.

147 Prov. 17.9; 19.11; 22.3.

148 Prov. 14.30; 17.27; 29.11.

149 Prov. 14.29; 15.18; 25.28.

150 Prov. 13.10.

151 Prov. 10.19; 11.12; 13.3; 15.2; 18.2; 18.6; 29.22.

152 Prov. 20.5.

153 Prov. 27.17.

154 Prov. 12.16.

155 Prov. 18.13.

156 Prov. 15.23; 25.11.

157 Prov. 12.23; 13.16; 25.15.

158 Prov. 19.2; 21.5.

159 Prov. 14.15.

160 Prov. 11.14; 14.17; 15.22; 20.18.

161 Prov. 1.5; 8.12; 22.29.

162 Prov. 24.5, 6; cf. 12.8; 15.24; 16.22; 21.22.

163 Prov. 13.13; 13.18; 25.12.

164 Prov. 15.12; 16.21; 22.17–21.

165 Prov. 6.6–11; 10.4; 10.26; 12.27; 18.9; 19.15; 19.24; 20.4; 20.13; 22.13; 24.30–34.

166 Prov. 16.15; 22.29.

6 THE LITERATURE OF THE SCRIBES

1 See R. B. Y. Scott, 'The Study of the Widsom Literature', *Interpretation*, XXIV.1 (1970), pp. 20–45; S. Terrien, 'Quelques remarques sue les affinités de Job avec le Deutéro-Esaïe', *Supplements to V.T.*, XV (1966), pp. 295–310; S. Talmon, '"Wisdom" in the Book of Esther', *V.T.*, XIII (1963), pp. 419–55; Moshe Weinfeld, *Deuteronomy and the Deuteronomic School* (1972), pp. 244–319; S. Mowinckel, 'Psalms and Widsom', *Supplements to V.T.*, III (1955), pp. 205–24; E. W. Heaton, *The Hebrew Kingdoms* (1968), pp. 165–96, *The Book of Daniel* (1956), pp. 32–47.

2 J. L. Crenshaw, 'Method in determining wisdom influence upon "historical" literature', *J.B.L.*, LXXXVIII (1969), pp. 129–42.

3 See pp. 121–26; cf., for example, J. William Whedbee, *Isaiah and Wisdom* (1971), with bibliography.

4 Gen. 37–50; see G. von Rad, *The Problem of the Hexateuch and Other Essays* (1966), pp. 292–300; *Genesis* (1961), pp. 428–34.

5 Gen. 38; 46.6–27; 48; 49.

6 R. de Vaux, *Histoire ancienne d'Israël* (1971), pp. 277–303.

7 Gen. 37.5–11; 40.1–41.32.

8 The two versions have been analysed recently by Donald B. Redford in *A Study of the Biblical Story of Joseph, Supplements to V.T.*, XX (1970). Though he concludes that the 'Jacob–Reuben' version constitutes the original story and was written *c.* 650–425 BC, it is significant that his arguments for this late date, on the evidence of vocabulary and the 'Egyptian colouring' of the story, leave the 'Israel–Judah' version virtually untouched. For this and other reasons, the present writer adheres to the view he expressed over twenty years ago that it is the 'Jacob–Reuben' version (corresponding to the so-called 'E' narrative) which is the later expansion; see E. W. Heaton, *E.T.*, 59 (1947), pp. 134–36.

9 Gen. 45.8; see pp. 49–50; cf. R. de Vaux, *op. cit.*, pp. 282–86.

10 *A.N.E.T.*, pp. 18–22; Erman, *A.E.*, pp. 14–29.

11 *A.N.E.T.*, pp. 23–25; Erman, *A.E.*, pp. 150–61.

12 Gen. 39.7–23; cf. Donald B. Redford, *op. cit.*, p. 93.

13 J. L. Crenshaw, *op. cit.*, p. 136; J. M. Plumley, *D.O.T.T.*, p. 171.

14 Gen. 39.8, 9.

15 Prov. 2.16–19; 5.1–23; 6.20–35; 7.6–27; 9.13–18; see pp. 117–18, 125.

16 *A.N.E.T.*, p. 24*b*; Erman, *A.E.*, p. 153; Gen. 39.21–23.

17 Gen. 45.5, 8; 50.20.

18 See pp. 119–20.

19 William C. Hayes, *C.A.H.*, vol. I, chap. XX (1961), p. 64.

20 G. Posener, in J. R. Harris (ed.), *The Legacy of Egypt* (1971), p. 240.

21 Gen. 37.2.

22 Gen. 41.34, 41–46.

23 R. A. Caminos, *L.E.M.*, pp. 4–5, 7, 15, 221, 293, 296; *A.N.E.T.*, p. 259*a*.

24 Gen. 44.1–17.

25 Prov. 21.5.

26 Gen. 43.30, 31; cf. 45.1.

27 Gen. 45.1–15; 46.29.

28 Prov. 12.16; 19.11; cf. 14.29, 30; 17.9; 24.29; cf.

R. de Vaux, *op. cit.*, pp. 281–82; see pp. 117–21.

29 R. A. Caminos, *L.E.M.*, pp. 419–21.

30 Gen 44.18–34.

31 R. de Vaux, *op. cit.*, pp. 282–94; Donald B. Redford, *op. cit.*, pp. 189–243; Tryggve N. D. Mettinger, *op. cit.*, pp. 76–79; 152–54. Note especially: the names Potiphar – 'He whom Re gives' (Gen. 39.1), Zaphenathpaneah – 'God speaks and he lives' (41.45); and Asenath – 'Belonging to (the goddess) Neith' (41.45); Joseph's death at 110 years (50.22, 26); and (less certainly) the cry 'Bow the knee' (41.43). On the ideal life-span for Egyptians, we may compare a New Kingdom letter addressed to a high official: 'May you complete 110 years upon earth', R. A. Caminos, *L.E.M.*, p. 143; cf. Erman, *A.E.*, p. 213; *A.N.E.T.*, p. 414*b*, n. 33; R. de Vaux, *op. cit.*, p. 293.

32 G. Posener, *Littérature et politique dans l'Égypte de la XIIᵉ dynastie* (1956), pp. 87–115.

33 II Sam. 8.15; cf. II Sam. 19.20; I Kgs. 11.28; see R. de Vaux, *op. cit.*, pp. 167, 295–96, 509–10, 589–90.

34 I Kgs. 4.25; cf. 4.20; see R. de Vaux, *op. cit.*, p. 291.

35 II Sam. 9.1–20.26 with I Kgs. 1.1–2.46, excluding the annalistic material in II Sam. 10.1–11.1 and 12.26–31.

36 I Kgs. 2.46; see R. N. Whybray, *The Succession Narrative* (1968).

37 *A.N.E.T.*, pp. 418–19; Erman, *A.E.*, pp. 72–74; G. Posener, *op. cit.*, pp. 61–86.

38 *A.N.E.T.*, pp. 444–46; Erman, *A.E.*, pp. 110–15; see G. Posener, *op. cit.*, pp. 21–60. For the name 'Neferty' instead of 'Nefer-rohu', see *A.N.E.T.*, p. 444, n. 1.

39 *A.N.E.T.*, pp. 18–22; Erman, *A.E.*, pp. 14–29; see pp. 132–33.

40 Ian Watt, *The Rise of the Novel* (1963).

41 G. J. Toomer, in J. R. Harris (ed.), *op. cit.*, pp. 38, 45.

42 G. Posener, in J. R. Harris (ed.), *op. cit.*, pp. 251–52.

43 Ian Watt, *op. cit.*, p. 87.

44 Erich Auerbach (trans. Willard R. Trask), *Mimesis* (1953), pp. 17–18.

45 G. Posener, *op. cit.*, pp. 32, 49–52, 65, 96–98; Cyril Aldred, *C.A.H.*, vol. II, chap. XIX (1971), pp. 47–48.

46 II Sam. 13.3, 32, 33; 13.1–22; 14.1–20; 18.19–30; 9.5–13; 19.24–30; 19.31–40; 16.5–14; 19.18–23; 20.14–22.

47 II Sam. 15.16; 16.20–22; 20.3.

48 II Sam. 15.13–23.

49 II Sam. 16.1–4.

50 II Sam. 17.15–22.

51 II Sam. 18.19–30.

52 See also II Sam. 11.22–25; 13.1–7; 13.23–27; 13.30, 31; 14.1–20; 15.7–9; I Kgs. 1.41, 42.

53 II Sam. 11.4; 11.6; 11.14; 11.18, 19; 11.22; 11.25; 11.27; 13.7; 13.30; 14.3, 19; 14.21, 24; 14.29, 32, 33; 15.10; 15.13; 15.27, 28; 15.35–37; 16.3; 17.15–22; 18.10; 18.19–33; 19.11; I Kgs. 1.11–14; 1.42; 1.51; 2.18; 2.28–31; 2.41.

54 Ptahhotep, *A.N.E.T.*, p. 413*a*; Erman, *A.E.*, pp. 58, 71. The duties of a messenger are described in *B.A.R.*, II, § 682.

55 Ptahhotep, *A.N.E.T.*, p. 414*a*; Erman, *A.E.*, p. 61; see pp. 117–18.

56 II Sam. 16.20–17.14; for the cliché 'as the sand for multitude', cf. R. A. Caminos, *L.E.M.*, p. 165; Erman, *A.E.*, p. 212 and see p. 27.

57 *Two Brothers*, see pp. 133–35; *Sinuhe*, see pp. 132–33; *Wenamun*, see pp. 28–29.

58 *A.N.E.T.*, pp. 26–27; II Sam. 11.2–27; cf. 14.1–20; 18.19–33.

59 II Sam. 17.14; cf. 11.27; 12.24, 25.

60 II Sam. 15.26; 16.10–12; cf. 12.22, 23; Eccles. 3.10–15; 6.10–12; 7.13.

61 See pp. 119–20; cf. Prov. 15.3; 16.9; 16.33; 19.21; 20.24; 21.30, 31.

62 *A.N.E.T.*, p. 417*b*; Erman, *A.E.*, p. 82.

63 G. von Rad, *Old Testament Theology*, vol. I (1962), pp. 51–56, 312–17; *The Problem of the Hexateuch and Other Essays* (1966), pp. 176–204.

64 Num. 13.17–20; see pp. 112–14.

65 Gen. 12.1–3; 18.18; 26.4; 28.14; Num. 32.11; cf. Gen. 15.18; Num. 24.3–9; also see the dynastic formula of II Sam. 7.9, which is thought to have been borrowed from Egypt; cf. R. J. Williams, in J. R. Harris (ed.), *op. cit.*, p. 274.

66 R. E. Clements, *Abraham and David* (1967), pp. 47–60; cf. Moshe Weinfeld, *op. cit.*, pp. 74–81.

67 J. R. Porter, *Moses and Monarchy* (1963), cf. J. R. Porter, 'The Succession of Joshua', in J. I. Durham and J. R. Porter (ed.), *Proclamation and Presence* (1970), pp. 102–32.

68 Num. 24.15–19; cf. Gen. 27.29; 49.10.

69 G. von Rad, *The Problem of the Hexateuch and Other Essays* (1966), p. 167; H. Gese, 'The Idea of History in the Ancient Near East and the Old Testament', *Journal for Theology and the Church*, I (1965), p. 50.

70 *A.N.E.T.*, pp. 232–33; Erman, *A.E.*, pp. 52–54; cf. T. G. H. James, *C.A.H.*, vol. II, chap. VIII (1965), pp. 3–6; Alan H. Gardiner, *Egypt of the Pharaohs* (1961), pp. 165–68.

71 *A.N.E.T.*, pp. 233–34; *B.A.R.*, II, §§ 1–25, 80–82.

72 K. A. Kitchen, in M. Liverani (ed.), *La Siria nel Tardo Bronzo* (1969), p. 92.

73 W. Stevenson Smith, *The Art and Architecture of Ancient Egypt* (1958), p. 224.

74 Erman, *A.E.*, pp. 260–70; cf. *A.N.E.T.*, pp. 255–56.

75 Gen. 28.13–15.

76 H. Cazelles, 'Les Localisations de l'Exode', *R.B.*, LXII (1955), p. 364.

77 R. de Vaux, *op. cit.*, p. 341.

78 Exod. 14.10–14, 24, 30, 31; cf. Josh. 11.1–9; Prov. 21.31.

79 The concept of 'Holy War' in Old Testament literature is generally, but probably erroneously, held to derive

from Israel's 'tribal' ancestry; cf. R. de Vaux, *op. cit.*, pp. 429–31; G. von Rad, *Studies in Deuteronomy* (1953), pp. 45–49; Moshe Weinfeld, *op. cit.*, pp. 238–39.

80 See G. von Rad, *Genesis* (1961), p. 24; *Old Testament Theology*, vol. I (1962), pp. 50–56, 157–58; *The Problem of the Hexateuch and Other Essays* (1966), pp. 68–74, 176–204, 292–300. B. S. Childs has ascribed the story of Moses' birth (Exod. 2.1–10) to the same circles as the Joseph Story; see 'The Birth of Moses', *J.B.L.*, LXXXIV (1965), pp. 109–22.

81 Gen. 18.1–33; cf. II Sam. 13.1–22; 14.1–20.

82 Gen. 24.1–67; I Kgs. 1.1–53; cf. Gen. 27.1.

83 As David is blamed for having failed to do (I Kgs. 1.6); cf. Gen. 27.1–45.

84 *A.N.E.T.*, pp. 420–21; Erman, *A.E.*, pp. 234–42; see pp. 118–19.

85 Gen. 24.3, 4, 15, 16, 21, 27, 33, 34, 50, 51, 67. Physical beauty is a constant theme of this scribal literature. The Joseph Story: Gen. 39.6; the Succession Story: II Sam. 11.2; 13.1; 14.25; 14.27; I Kgs. 1.6; the Yahwist's History: Gen. 6.2; 24.16; 26.7; 29.17; cf. Exod. 2.2.

86 Gen. 2.4–3.19.

87 W. G. Lambert, 'A New Look at the Babylonian Background of Genesis', *J.T.S.*, XVI.2 (1965), pp. 287–300.

88 Gen. 3.8; R. A. Caminos, *L.E.M.*, p. 164; Erman, *A.E.*, pp. 211–12; 237–38; *A.N.E.T.*, p. 420*b*.

89 Gen. 2.10–14.

90 Gen. 2.6; cf. Ecclus. 39.22 (Hebrew has 'like a Nile'); see 'Hymn to the Nile', *A.N.E.T.*, pp. 372–73; Erman, *A.E.*, pp. 146–49.

91 Gen. 2.7; cf. Isa. 29.16; 45.9; 64.8; Jer. 18.4; Job 10.8, 9; 33.6; Ecclus. 33.13; Wisdom 15.7; *A.N.E.T.*, p. 424*b*; *B.A.R.*, II, §§ 202, 203; cf. S. G. F. Brandon, *Creation Legends of the Ancient Near East* (1963), p. 60; A. M. Blackman, *Luxor and its Temples* (1923), pp. 162–70.

92 Gen. 2.7; *Hymn to Aten*, line 44 ('Who givest breath to sustain all that he has made'), cf. Ps. 104.29, 30; *A.N.E.T.*, p. 370*b*; *D.O.T.T.*, pp. 142–50; cf. A. Barucq, *L'Expression de la louange divine et de la prière dans la Bible et en Égypte* (1962), pp. 303, 316–21.

93 Gen. 2.20; see p. 114.

94 Gen. 2.21. There is, how-

ever, no explicit evidence in the Egyptian surgical papyri to illuminate the Yahwist's language; see J. R. Harris (ed.), *op. cit.*, pp. 112–37.

95 See pp. 117–18, 124–25; cf. Cyril Aldred, *op. cit.*, pp. 48–49.

96 Gen. 2.17; 3.5, 22; see W. Malcolm Clark, 'A Legal Background of the Yahwist's use of "Good and Evil" in Genesis 2–3', *J.B.L.*, LXXXVIII (1969), pp. 266–78.

97 II Sam. 14.17, 20; see H. Duesberg and I. Fransen, *Les Scribes inspirés* (1966), pp. 105–106.

98 I Kgs. 3.9; cf. II Sam. 19.27.

99 Gen. 24.50.

100 Gen. 31.24, 29; cf. II Sam. 13.22.

101 Gen. 3.5, 22; *Amenemope* 21.15; *A.N.E.T.*, p. 424*a*; see pp. 117–20.

102 Gen. 3.17–19; see pp. 104–107.

103 The following observations are based on David Daube, 'The Culture of Deuteronomy', ORITA, University of Ibadan, III.1 (1969), pp. 27–52. Daube refers to the Yahwist's creation narrative as 'a wisdom story'.

104 Gen. 2.25; 3.7–12; see, above, note 15; cf. J. Blen-

kinsopp, 'Theme and Motif in the Succession History (2 Sam. XI.2ff) and the Yahwist Corpus', *Supplements to V.T.*, XV (1966), pp. 44–57.

105 The shame motive underlies the suicide of Ahithophel (II Sam. 17.23), with which we may compare the Egyptian practice of punishment by enforced suicide; see *B.A.R.*, IV, §§ 444, 446–50, 452, 454, 456; *A.N.E.T.*, pp. 215–16. It is also found in Deut. 22.13–21; 23.12–14; 24.10, 11; 25.3; 25.5–10; 25.11, 12. For the idea that God's reputation depends on Israel's fortunes 'in the sight of the nations', see Deut. 9.27, 28; Ezek. 5.4–8; 5.14, 15; 20.9, 14, 22, 42–44; 36.22, 23, 31, 32, 36; 37.28.

7 SOLOMON'S CULTURAL MILIEU

1 John Gray, *The Canaanites* (1964); A. S. Kapelrud, *The Ras Shamra Discoveries and the Old Testament* (1965).

2 Donald Harden, *The Phoenicians* (1962), pp. 115–23; Mitchell Dahood, 'The Phoenician Contribution to Biblical Wisdom Literature', in William A. Ward (ed.), *The Role of the Phoenicians in the Interaction of Mediterranean Civilizations* (1968), pp. 123–48; cf. 'Phoenician Elements in Isaiah 52.13–53.12', in Hans

Goedicke (ed.), *Near Eastern Studies* (1971), pp. 63–73.

3 W. F. Albright in G. E. Wright (ed.), *The Bible and the Ancient Near East* (1961), p. 351.

4 I Kgs. 5.18.

5 *E.A.*, 147, *A.N.E.T.*, p. 484, n. 2; K. A. Kitchen, 'Inter-relations of Egypt and Syria', in M. Liverani (ed.), *La Siria nel Tardo Bronzo* (1969), pp. 88–89.

6 Alan H. Gardiner, *Egypt of the Pharaohs* (1961), p. 310; *A.N.E.T.*, p. 27a; cf. R. de Vaux, *Histoire ancienne d'Israël* (1971), pp. 75–78; Nina Jidejian, *Byblos Through the Ages* (1968), pp. 15–73.

7 K. A. Kitchen, *op. cit.*, pp. 87–88; R. de Vaux, *op. cit.*, p. 118; *A.N.E.T.*, pp. 17–18, 23–25; Erman, *A.E.*, pp. 150–61.

8 *A.N.E.T.*, pp. 476 n. 23, 477 n. 41.

9 Erman, *A.E.*, p. 241.

10 John Gray, *The Legacy of Canaan, Supplements to V.T.*, V (1957), pp. 189–216.

11 See p. 121.

12 R. de Vaux, *op. cit.*, pp. 294, 310–13, 341.

13 J. M. A. Janssen, 'Fonction-naires sémites au service de l'Égypte', *C.E.*, 26 (1951),

pp. 50–62; R. de Vaux, *op. cit.*, pp. 98, 284–86.

14 Margaret S. Drower, *C.A.H.*, vol. II, chap. X, part I (1970), p. 55; cf. W. F. Albright, *A.N.E.T.*, p. 486, n. 11.

15 *E.A.*, 296.16–29, trans. S. A. B. Mercer, *The Tell El-Amarna Tablets*, vol. II (1939), p. 735; *B.A.R.*, II, § 467; *A.N.E.T.*, p. 239a; R. de Vaux, *op. cit.*, p. 98; Margaret S. Drower, *op. cit.*, pp. 7, 52–53, 59.

16 *E.A.*, 5.20; 14, col. II.7, col. IV.8; 22, col. II.23, 43; 25, col. II.56.

17 I Kgs. 5.18; 7.13, 14.

18 I Kgs. 16.29–34.

19 J. W. Crowfoot, K. M. Kenyon, E. L. Sukenik, *Samaria-Sebaste* I: *The Buildings at Samaria* (1942), pp. 5–9.

20 I Kgs. 22.39.

21 Kathleen M. Kenyon, *Royal Cities of the Old Testament* (1971), pp. 47–49, 61, 76–89; see pp. 82–83.

22 I Sam. 8.10–17; cf. I. Mendelsohn, 'Samuel's Denunciation of Kingship in the Light of Akkadian Documents from Ugarit', *B.A.S.O.R.*, 143 (1956), pp. 17–22.

23 Josh. 11.10; *E.A.*, 227, 148;

cf. Margaret S. Drower, *op. cit.*, pp. 50–65.

24 See William C. Hayes, *C.A.H.*, vol. I, chap. XX (1961), p. 43; G. Posener, *C.A.H.*, vol. I, chap. XXI (1965), p. 16.

25 *A.N.E.T.*, pp. 27, 28.

26 W. F. Albright, *C.A.H.*, vol. II, chap. XX (1966), pp. 4, 13.

27 Josh. 15.63; II Sam. 5.6–9; see K. M. Kenyon, *Jerusalem* (1967), pp. 16–53.

28 *E.A.*, 287; cf. *E.A.*, 286, 288; *A.N.E.T.*, pp. 487–89.

29 See pp. 37–40.

30 G. Buccellati, *Cities and Nations of Ancient Syria* (1967), p. 39.

31 *E.A.*, 108, 139, 148, 149, 151, 238.

32 Judg. 4.2, 24; cf. R. de Vaux, *op. cit.*, pp. 602–605; Y. Yadin, *Hazor* (1972), pp. 129, 132.

33 *A.N.E.T.*, pp. 234–38; *B.A.R.*, II, §§ 391–443.

34 William G. Denver and others, 'Further Excavations at Gezer, 1967–1971', *B.A.*, XXXIV.4 (1971), pp. 110–11.

35 Frances M. James, *The Iron Age at Beth-Shan* (1966).

36 W. A. Ward, in Frances M. James, *op. cit.*, pp. 161–79.

37 H. O. Thompson, 'Tell el-Husn–Biblical Beth-shan', *B.A.*, XXX.4 (1967), pp. 110–35; *Mekal God of Beth-Shan* (1970); A. Rowe, *Four Canaanite Temples* (1940), p. 7, fig. 3.

38 R. de Vaux, *op. cit.*, p. 477.

39 Frances M. James, *op. cit.*, p. 138.

40 I Kgs. 11.14–22, 25.

41 I Kgs. 3.1; 7.8; 9.15–17, 24.

42 A. Malamat, 'Aspects of the Foreign Policies of David and Solomon', *J.N.E.S.*, XXII.1 (1963), pp. 1–17.

43 J. Černý, *C.A.H.*, vol. II, chap. XXXV (1965), pp. 53–54.

Chronological table (all the dates *circa* B C)

EGYPT	EGYPTIAN WRITINGS	PALESTINE
		3200–2100 Early Bronze Age
2686–2181 OLD KINGDOM		
2613 Sneferu		
	2350 *Instruction of Ptahhotep*	
	2100 *Instruction for Merikare*	
2050–1786 MIDDLE KINGDOM		2100–1550 Middle Bronze Age
1991–1786 *Twelfth Dynasty*	1990 *Prophecy of Neferty*	
1991–1962 Ammenemes I	1960 *Instruction of Ammenemes I*	
	1960 *Book of Kemit*	
1971–1928 Sesostris I	1960 *Satire of the Trades*	
	1960 *Story of Sinuhe*	1800 Beginning of the 'Patriarchal Period'
	1786–1633 'Ramesseum Onomasticon'	
1750–1550 Hyksos Period		1550–1200 Late Bronze Age
1567–1085 NEW KINGDOM		
1567–1320 *Eighteenth Dynasty*		
1570–1546 Amosis		
1546–1526 Amenophis I		
1525–1512 Tuthmosis I		
1512–1504 Tuthmosis II		
1504–1450 Tuthmosis III		
1450–1425 Amenophis II		Campaigns of Amenophis II
1425–1417 Tuthmosis IV		
1417–1379 Amenophis III	1387–1362 Amarna Letters	
1379–1362 Amenophis IV (Akhenaten)		
1361–1352 Tutankhamun		
1348–1320 Horemheb		

EGYPT	EGYPTIAN WRITINGS	PALESTINE
1320–1085 RAMESSIDE PERIOD		
1320–1200 *Nineteenth Dynasty*		
1320–1318 Ramesses I		
1318–1304 Sethos I		Campaigns of Sethos I
1304–1237 Ramesses II	1304–1237 Hori's *Satirical Letter*	Campaigns of Ramesses II
1236–1223 Merneptah	1225 Manuscript of the *Tale of the Two Brothers*	1225 Period of the Exodus
1216–1210 Sethos II		
		1200–900 Early Iron Age
1200–1085 *Twentieth Dynasty*		
1198–1166 Ramesses III		1200–1020 Period of the Judges
1166–1160 Ramesses IV	1166 Great Harris Papyrus	1190 Philistine settlement
1160–1156 Ramesses V		
1156–1148 Ramesses VI	? *Instruction of Ani*	
1148–1147 Ramesses VII		
1147–1140 Ramesses VIII		
1140–1121 Ramesses IX		
1121–1113 Ramesses X	1100 *Instruction of Amenemope*	
1113–1085 Ramesses XI	1113–1085 *Journey of Wenamun*	
		ISRAELITE MONARCHY
1085–935 *Twenty-first Dynasty*	1085 Amenope's *Onomasticon*	1020–1000 Saul
?950 Siamun		1000–960 David
		960–930 Solomon
		930 Disruption of the Kingdom

List of illustrations: sources and references

PLATES

1 Syrians present gifts to the Pharaoh, painting. Egypt, Thebes. *See* Nina M. Davies and Alan H. Gardiner, *Ancient Egyptian Paintings*, vol. I, Plate XLII and vol. III, pp. 84–85. Photo Peter Clayton.

2 The dissolute Amenophis III and Queen Tiy, stela. London, British Museum. *See A.N.E.P.*, fig. 400.

3 Social life in the reign of Amenophis III, painting. Egypt, Thebes. *See* Nina M. Davies and Alan H. Gardiner, *Ancient Egyptian Paintings*, vol. II, Plate LXI and vol. III, pp. 116–17.

4 Commemorative reliefs of Ramesses III. Egypt, Medinet Habu. *See Later Historical Records of Ramses III: Medinet Habu II*, Plate 61. Photo Oriental Institute, Chicago.

5 The 'Blessing of Ptah', relief. Egypt, Medinet Habu. *See Later Historical Records of Ramses III: Medinet Habu II*, Plate 105; text in William F. Edgerton and John A. Wilson, *Historical Records of Ramses III*, pp. 119–29. Photo Oriental Institute, Chicago.

6 The Great Harris Papyrus. London, British Museum.

7 Queen Hatshepsut's ships being loaded in Punt, relief. Egypt, Deir el Bahari. *See* Irmgard Woldering, *The Arts of Egypt*, pp. 123–24 and E. Naville, *The Temple of Deir el Bahari*, Part III, Plate LXXIV and p. 15. Photo Egyptian Exploration Society.

8 The universal dominion of Ramesses III, relief. Egypt, Medinet Habu. *See Later Historical Records of Ramses III: Medinet Habu II*, Plate 102; text in William F. Edgerton and John A. Wilson, *Historical Records of Ramses III*, pp. 111–13. Photo Oriental Institute of Chicago.

9 Syrians grovelling at the feet of the Pharaoh, painting. Egypt, Thebes. *See* Nina M. Davies and Alan H. Gardiner, *Ancient Egyptian Paintings*, vol. II, Plate LX and vol. III, p. 115.

10 Scribes registering geese brought as tax, painting. Egypt, Thebes. London, British Museum. *See* Nina M. Davies and Alan H. Gardiner, *Ancient Egyptian Paintings*, vol. II, Plate LXVII and vol. III, pp. 128–29.

11 'Gold of Ophir': an ostracon from Tell Qasileh. Tel Aviv,

List of illustrations

First Merchant Venturers, p. 63, fig. 69.

25 The king of Byblos on his sphinx-throne, stone sarcophagus from Byblos. *See* H. Frankfort, *The Art and Architecture of the Ancient Orient*, pp. 271–72.

26 Lion-and-sphinx throne of Ramesses III, relief. Egypt, Medinet Habu. *See Festival Scenes of Ramses III: Medinet Habu IV*, Plate 197 and J. Vandier, *Manuel d'Archéologie Égyptienne*, vol. IV, pp. 354–63.

27 Ivory of a cow suckling its calf from Nimrud. *See* M. E. L. Mallowan, *Nimrud* II, p. 520, Plate VI and fig. 425. Photo courtesy Professor Sir Max Mallowan and British School of Archaeology, Iraq.

28 Ivory plaque of the mother-goddess from Ugarit. *See* C. F. A. Schaeffer, *Syria* XXXI (1954), pp. 51–59, Plate VIII.

29 Egyptian musicians at a banquet, painting. Egypt, Thebes. *See* Nina M. Davies and Alan H. Gardiner, *Ancient Egyptian Paintings*, vol. I, Plate XXXVII and vol. III, pp. 76–77.

30 Court musicians on an ivory from Nimrud. *See* M. E. L. Mallowan, *Nimrud I*, p. 216, fig. 168. Photo courtesy Sir Max Mallowan and British School of Archaeology, Iraq.

31 A satirical Egyptian painting. Cairo, Egyptian Museum. On the satirical vein of Egyptian art, *see* W. Stevenson Smith, *The Art and Architecture of Ancient Egypt*, pp. 235–36; also Edward L. B. Terrace and Henry G. Fischer, *Treasures of the Cairo Museum*, pp. 149–52.

32 The Master of the Horse is honoured by the Pharaoh, relief. Egypt, Amarna. *See* N. de Garis Davies, *The Rock Tombs of El Amarna*, vol. VI, pp. 21–22, Plate XXIX.

33 An Egyptian official supervises the registering of the harvest, painting. Egypt, Thebes. *See* Nina M. Davies and Alan H. Gardiner, *Ancient Egyptian Paintings*, vol. I, Plate LI and vol. III, pp. 100–101.

34 An Egyptian scribe and his family enjoying a hunting party, painting. Egypt, Thebes. *See* Nina M. Davies and Alan H. Gardiner, *Ancient Egyptian Paintings*, vol. I, Plate XLVII and vol. III, pp. 94–95.

35 An Egyptian scribe and the god of writing. *See* Edward L. B. Terrace and Henry G. Fischer, *Treasures of the Cairo Museum*, pp. 129–32.

36 An elegant style of life objectively portrayed, painting. Egypt, Thebes. New York, Metropolitan Museum of Art. *See* N. de Garis Davies, *Two Ramesside Tombs at Thebes*, Plate XVIII; also W. Stevenson Smith, *The Art and Architecture of Ancient Egypt*, pp. 130, 225.

37 A king and queen in their

List of illustrations

Beth-Shean. Egypt, Beth-Shean. *See* the commentary by William A. Ward in Frances M. James, *The Iron Age at Beth-Shan*, pp. 167–69 and figs. 92.1 and 93.1. Photo University Museum, University of Pennsylvania.

52 Stela of Sethos I from Beth-Shean. For a translation of the inscription, *see A.N.E.T.*, pp. 253–54.

53 Stela of Ramesses II from Beth-Shean. For a translation of a brief extract, *see A.N.E.T.*, p. 255.

FIGURES

1 Foreigners submit to the Pharaoh, painting. Egypt, Thebes. *See* Nina M. Davies and Alan H. Gardiner, *Ancient Egyptian Paintings*, vol. II, Plate LVIII and vol. III, pp. 112–13.

2 The battle of Ramesses III against the Philistines and the 'Peoples of the Sea', relief. Egypt, Medinet Habu. *See Earlier Historical Records of Ramses III: Medinet Habu I*, Plate 37 and Y. Yadin, *The Art of Warfare in Biblical Lands*, pp. 340–41.

3 The Kingdom of David, map drawn by Harold King.

4 The Canaanite King of Megiddo, ivory plaque. Jordan, Palestine Archaeological Museum. *See A.N.E.P.*, fig. 332.

5 Solomon's administrative districts and fortified cities. Map drawn by Harold King.

6, 7 Syrian and Nubian slaves making bricks in Egypt, painting. Egypt, Thebes. *See* N. de Garis Davies, *The Tomb of Rekh-mi-re at Thebes*, vol. I, p. 55 and vol. II, Plate 58.

8 The Ancient Near East and its trade routes. Map drawn by Harold King.

9 Plan of the Solomonic gate at Megiddo. *See* Y. Yadin, *I.E.J.*, 8.2 (1958), pp. 80–86, fig. 4; *Hazor*, pp. 138, 147–61. Redrawn by Sarah Lillywhite.

10 Plan of the Solomonic gate and casemate-wall at Hazor. *See* Y. Yadin, *I.E.J.*, 8.2 (1958), pp. 80–86, fig. 2; *Hazor*, pp. 135–38, figs. 30, 31. Redrawn by Sarah Lillywhite.

11 Reconstructed plan of the Solomonic gate at Gezer. *See* Y. Yadin, *I.E.J.*, 8.2 (1958), pp. 80–86, fig. 3. Redrawn by Sarah Lillywhite.

12 The 'southern palace' in Solomonic Megiddo. *See* D. Ussishkin, *I.E.J.*, 16.3 (1966), pp. 174–86, fig. 4. Redrawn by Sarah Lillywhite.

13 A North Syrian palace at Zinjirili. *See* D. Ussishkin, *I.E.J.*, 16.3 (1966), pp. 174–86, fig. 2. Redrawn by Sarah Lillywhite.

14 The 'House of the Forest of Lebanon', drawing by Th. A. Busink, *Der Tempel von Jerusalem*, I. Band, *Der Tempel Salomos*, Abb. 37.

Index